Between Two Homes: A Coparenting Handbook

Bradley S. Craig

LMSW-IPR, CFLE

This book is intended for educational purposes only. It is not intended to constitute mental-health therapy, give information about specific mental-health disorders, or provide information about medications to treat mental-health disorders. Readers are encouraged to discuss specific mental-health questions with a licensed mental-health therapist. This book is not intended to constitute legal advice. For answers to specific legal questions, please consult with a licensed attorney.

BTH Publications may be ordered through booksellers or by contacting:

Between Two Homes®
PO Box 1353
Mineola, TX 75773
www.betweentwohomes.com
(800) 239-3971

ACKNOWLEDGMENTS

I could not have learned and grown in this field without the contributions, insights, and dedication of my professional peers. The Association of Family and Conciliation Courts is the leading organization setting standards of practice for this profession, and I have spent many hours in various workshops at state and international conferences learning from leaders in the profession of helping families through transitions. In addition, I have learned a great deal from the members of the North Texas Families in Transition professional workgroup, the collaborative practice groups I have been a member of, and the attorneys and judges I have had the fortune to practice with and serve.

I would be remiss to not acknowledge the families I have had the privilege to work with. Through their experiences, I have gained far more insight than literature, my own experiences, or lectures could provide me. Hearing both the pain and joy of families raising children between two homes helps me continue my course of work in this field. Despite frustrations and occasional setbacks, the continued feedback from parents about the impact of my parenting classes and other services reminds me why I do what I do.

DEDICATION

This book is dedicated to my loving wife, Patty, my sons, Todd and Scott, and my mother. It is also dedicated to my mentor Dr. Don Granvold, who left this world too soon and who encouraged me… publish, publish, publish.

CONTENTS

PART 1 – ADULT ISSUES

AUTHOR'S NOTE

First, thank you for purchasing this book. You may be a parent, a relative, an interested party, or a professional working with families raising children between two homes. Whatever the reason for your interest, my hope is that this book will provide you with insights to help improve the quality of life for children growing up in one or more homes.

My own parents divorced when I was ten years old, and my passion for working in this field stems from that experience. I began professionally specializing in working with families raising children between two homes in 1993, when I was hired by Family Court Services in Tarrant County, Texas, as a caseworker. I had the good fortune to interact with many skilled professionals, including judges and attorneys, who helped me gain a different perspective of the family-law process and how the system at times truly protects children. What I did not experience (with a few exceptions) were colleagues who were burnt out, supervisors who were there for a check, judges who did not care, or attorneys who were willing to destroy families for the right price. Instead, I experienced colleagues who cared about families and were willing to mentor me, supervisors who cared about improving my quality of work, judges who were creative and sincerely vested in the best interests of children, and a vast majority of attorneys who were solution focused and collaborative. I was extremely fortunate to have had these experiences.

Other than a few cases that I was able to mediate, most of the work I did for the county was forensic investigations on behalf of and at the direction of various family-court judges. My job was to complete custody evaluations, where I made recommendations to the court regarding parenting-time arrangements for children. I enjoyed meeting and learning about the families, making recommendations, and even at times taking the stand to defend my investigations. During my investigations, parents would tell me the truth, tell me half-truths (mostly regarding their strengths and the deficits of the other family members), or outright lie to me. My job was to ferret out the truth of these stories by interviewing the parents and children, getting information from family and friends, and gathering professional records, such as school transcripts and psychological and medical records of the parents and children.

Parents often do not realize how easy it is to gather records and instead believe a custody evaluator will accept just the "he said, she said" version of the story. But by digging deep into records and interviewing other sources, an investigator can determine the truth, or the lack thereof. I was often able to prove whether the stories parents shared with me were factual, manipulated, or clearly deceptive. I had the honor to prepare reports that helped guide judges to produce orders in the best interests of the children.

Over time, however, I realized I was negatively affecting (even if only temporarily) the lives of the most important individuals when families are in litigation: the children. When parents would come to my office, so often it was clear they were not acting as "mom and dad" but instead as "petitioner and respondent." Many times they would share with me how rotten their coparent was as a person and what a bad parent that coparent was, and they would then want me to talk to all their friends and relatives who shared their point of view. After hearing their stories, I would then interview their friends, families, and children and gather all their private records, which would later be shared in a courtroom full of strangers.

I noticed some strange byproducts of this process. As the dust was settling during the investigation, the parents would typically begin working together, if only because I was evaluating them both as a parenting unit. However, once I released my custody evaluation full of all the negative things they were saying about each other; what their friends, relatives, and professionals were saying about them; and what their private records revealed, any positive progress made from the time I started the study until the date it was released vanished, and the distance between the parents was greater than before the investigation began.

I realized, with the exception of cases involving abuse, neglect, or severe mental illness, the ones paying the price for this regression are the children, the very people the system seeks to protect. So I decided to leave the county and begin interventions to help families work together to successfully raise their children between two homes. One of my first steps was to design a coparenting class, which is the basis for this book.

My goal in writing this book, and in all the services I currently provide, is to help adults work together as a family. I want families to keep the power of the family in their hands. My goal is to shift parents from a litigation mindset to the business of coparenting, and ultimately to improve the quality of life for children growing up between two homes.

PART 1 – ADULT ISSUES

Chapter 1: What Is Coparenting?

"When both parents are working toward one common goal—
the children and the children's welfare—we have a much happier,
healthier family, even if they're not all living in the same home."
—*Barbara Nunneley, Attorney at Law*

I wrote this book to assist adults with raising their
children when two homes are involved. If you are one of
the adults caring for a child in this situation, my goal is to
provide you with new tools to help in your coparenting
relationship and offer insights regarding the needs of your
child.

Raising an emotionally healthy child between two homes
is extremely challenging. Nevertheless, one of the best
means to accomplish this is to develop a healthy coparenting
relationship. So what do I mean by coparenting?

"Coparenting" is a term used to describe adults working
together and sharing the duties of raising a child.
Coparenting happens when adults live in the same home,
but it also occurs when adults are raising children between
two or more homes.

This book focuses on the coparenting relationship when
a child is growing up between two or more homes, or when
the coparents are living in more than one home. This book
is not just for divorcing parents; it is designed to help
families raise children between two homes, no matter what
the situation.

Many circumstances can lead to a child growing up
between two homes:

- Divorce.
- The child is a product of a one-night stand or a casual
  relationship, and the parents never lived together.

- The parents lived together for a period but never married.
- The parents are a same-sex couple who do not reside in the same home any longer, if they ever did.
- Other relatives share one or both of the child's homes.

Likely, you are reading this book because you are thinking about separating, are going through a divorce, need a legal arrangement for your child, or have already been to court for matters regarding your child. Hopefully, stepparents, grandparents, other relatives, lovers, and other individuals involved in raising children between two homes will read this book to develop better tools for coparenting and to assist the coparents. It is also my hope that attorneys, judges, educators, and mental-health professionals will gain insights from this book and find this book to be a helpful resource for the families who receive their services.

This book is not just for divorcing parents, but because the vast majority of readers are divorcing couples, circumstances involving divorce are referenced the most. If you are not the biological or adoptive parents, please use some liberty in applying this content to your situation and your role in improving the life of a child growing up between two homes.

There are many studies detailing the significant changes in our society, such as the increased rate of divorce, increased cohabitation rates, and increased number of children born out of wedlock to parents who never lived together. (**Note**: For more information about the studies referenced here and elsewhere in this book, see the bibliography at the end.)

Estimates suggest:

- Three-quarters of divorced men and two-thirds of divorced women remarry.
- One third of children will live in cohabitating or remarried families.

- About forty-three percent of all marriages are remarriages for at least one of the adults.
- About fifty percent of all first marriages will eventually end in divorce (National Center for Health Statistics, 1995).
- About sixty-five percent of remarriages involve children from the prior marriage and form stepfamilies (Lugaila, 1992).
- Around 60 percent of all second marriages eventually end in divorce, often within the first five years (Cherlin, 2005).

These numbers do not reflect the vast number of children growing up between two homes for reasons other than divorce.

There are also ample studies regarding the needs of children growing up between two homes. One consistent theme in the research is that the single most important factor for a child to thrive beyond the change that led to two homes is the ability of the adults in both homes to work together in the best interests of the child. An African proverb states, "When elephants fight, the grass gets hurt." Research indicates that highly conflicted families create tremendous burdens on their children, while adults who are able to set their emotions aside and focus on their children's needs can create positive results for their children. (Amato, 2000; Clarke-Stewart and Brentano, 2006; Emery, 2004; Hetherington and Kelly, 2002; Kelly, 2007; Johnston, 1994.)

Coparenting is difficult. To coparent successfully, you must shift your mindset from "What do *I* want and what am *I* feeling?" to "What is best for *our* child?"

Successful coparenting involves not only sympathy for your child's experiences, but also empathy—in other words, trying to put yourself in your child's shoes. Coparenting is about respecting your child's right to have at least two emotionally healthy caregivers actively involved in his or her life, regardless of whether those caregivers are in an intimate relationship.

When you separate and divorce, you are ending a

romantic and/or sexual relationship with someone. But once you have a child, whether the result of a one-night stand, an adoption, or a twenty-year marriage, you have created a family unit for your child for the child's lifetime.

It is important to separate your feelings toward your coparent from the feelings you have or had about that person as your lover. A person may not be very skilled at intimate relationships, but may still be a fantastic parent. In other words, a bad spouse does not necessarily equal a bad parent. You can stop being lovers and you can stop being spouses, but once you have a child with someone **you never stop being a family**.

When you separate, you are not forming two families; instead, you are changing the layout of your child's one family. In the United States, a child's core family is often his or her parents. In some other cases and in some other countries, the norm is for other family members to serve in the role of primary caregivers to a child.

When the primary caregivers to a child do not live in the same home, there may be two homes, but the child still has one big family consisting of all the family members (both maternal and paternal). Coparenting is a part of the job of that family.

The goal of this book is to assist you in tackling this often difficult, sometimes confusing, but always important coparenting role in the life of your child.

This book:

- Teaches effective communication and conflict-resolution skills.
- Helps you increase your sensitivity to your child's needs.
- Helps you focus on present child-rearing and the development and maintenance of a two-home parenting environment.
- Teaches skills to work with your coparenting partner(s).
- Helps you recognize how your own actions might help or hurt the coparenting relationship.

4

Once you and your coparent have developed a successful coparenting relationship, your child should experience:

- Less conflict, less stress, and higher self-esteem.
- An increased likelihood of two parents actively involved in his or her life.
- Reduction in feeling the need to "pick sides" or be "loyal" to one parent over the other.
- The role-modeling of good communication and conflict-resolution skills.
- A reduced likelihood of involvement in high-risk behaviors.

Chapter 2: Steps to a Successful Coparenting Relationship

Steps to a successful coparenting relationship include:

- Rules for Coparenting
- Maintaining Healthy Boundaries
- Understanding Feelings Versus Actions
- Understanding Grief
- Taking Care of Yourself
- Maintaining a Coparenting Alliance
- Improving Communication
- Family-Friendly Language
- "I" Statements
- Increasing Your Chance of Being Heard
- Guidelines for Effective E-mail Communication
- Healthy Negotiation and Exploring Interests
- Making It All About Your Child

Step 1: Rules for Coparenting

1. **At all times**, the decisions made by the parents will be for your child's psychological, spiritual, and physical well-being and safety.
2. **Do** make and confirm parenting-time arrangements beforehand between the parents without involving your child.
3. **Do** notify each other in a timely manner of any need to deviate from the schedule between homes, including canceling time with your child, rescheduling, and punctuality.

4. **Do** communicate with your coparent and make similar rules in reference to discipline, routines, sleeping arrangements, and schedules between homes. *Appropriate* discipline should be exercised by mutually agreed upon adults.

5. **Do** keep your coparent informed of any scholastic, medical, psychiatric, or extracurricular activities or appointments of your child.

6. **Do** keep your coparent informed at all times of your address and telephone number. If you are out of town with your child, **do** provide your coparent the basic travel itinerary and a phone number so that you and your child may be reached in case of an emergency.

7. **Do** refer to your coparent as your child's "mother" or "father" in conversation, rather than using "my ex."

8. **Do not** talk negatively, or allow others to talk negatively, about the other parent, his or her family and friends, or his or her home within hearing range of your child. This includes belittling remarks, ridicule, or bringing up allegations, whether *valid or invalid*, about issues involving the adults in the coparenting relationship.

9. **Do not** question your child about your coparent, the activities of your coparent, or regarding your coparent's personal life. In other words, do not use your child to spy on the other parent.

10. **Do not** argue or have heated conversations when your child is present.

11. **Do not** try to "win your child over" at the expense of your child's other parent.

12. **Do not** schedule extracurricular activities for your child during the other parent's time without your coparent's consent. However, **do** work together to allow your child to be involved in such activities.

13. **Do not** involve your child in adult issues and conversations about custody, the court, or the other parent.

14. **Do not** ask your child where he or she wants to live.

15. **Do not** attempt to alienate your coparent from your child's life.
16. **Do not** allow stepparents or others to negatively alter or modify your relationship with your coparent.
17. **Do not** use phrases that draw your child into your issues or make your child feel guilty about the time spent with the other parent. **Do not** say "I miss you!" **Do** say, "I love you!"

Step 2: Maintaining Healthy Boundaries

One important concept in self-care, relationships, parenting, and coparenting is the understanding of healthy and unhealthy boundaries. Often families are entrenched in conflict because healthy boundaries are not recognized, established, or respected.

Fences, windows, houses, and walls are all examples of physical boundaries. Even your skin is an example of a boundary; it lets some things in, while keeping other things out.

As humans we experience psychological boundaries as well. Your need for personal space is an example of a psychological boundary, and that boundary may differ from one person to the next. Personal space defines where you end and someone else begins. For some individuals, having a person stand a few inches from them is comfortable, but another's personal space boundary may extend a few feet from him or her. Additionally, someone's personal space boundary may change, depending on the other person or people involved and the event within which that person is interacting.

Your individual psychological boundaries are shaped by your experiences, your ideas, your world view, and your beliefs. These factors influence your actions and choices, as well as whom you choose to be around. Early childhood experiences can greatly affect how boundaries play a part in your world. These invisible psychological boundaries affect how you think and act, from broad concepts such as right and wrong, to very personal experiences, such as who can touch you. For example, some readers may not have a problem at all if you happen to ask them a question while they're reading this book, while others may feel frustrated that you interrupted them while they're clearly in the middle of reading.

Your personal boundaries vary from one person to another and from one situation to another. In healthy relationships, your boundary with another person is flexible and safe. Maintaining healthy boundaries means recognizing and respecting your boundaries, while also recognizing and respecting the boundaries of others at different times, based on circumstances.

Respecting the boundaries of your child and your coparent involves recognizing that your child and your coparent have the same right to expect that their personal boundaries will be both respected and honored by you. Many times, being properly respectful involves accepting responsibility for any lies or poor behavior on your part by acknowledging what you've done and apologizing.

It may be difficult to know when you have crossed your coparent's boundaries, especially if he or she has not made those boundaries clear. However, there are obvious boundary violations. The law has defined some boundaries for us, such as privacy, safety, slander, and consent. Other examples include entering your coparent's personal space without his or her consent, such as showing up on his or her doorstep without permission, searching his or her computer, reading his or her texts, going through his or her belongings, posting on his or her online accounts, or stalking your coparent. Still more examples include withholding important information about your child (medical, extracurricular, or travel), spreading vindictive information about your coparent to others verbally or via the Internet, harassing your coparent verbally or in writing, and physically, sexually, or verbally abusing your coparent. More subtle forms of boundary crossing include denying or challenging your coparent or your child regarding his or her right to feel or believe a certain way.

There is a difference between assertive behaviors and

aggressive ones. Assertive communication respects boundaries by defining for others what is or is not acceptable for you. However, aggressive behaviors violate the boundaries of others. Aggressive behaviors include:

- **Obvious aggression**: Observable external behaviors that violate the rights of others. Typical of individuals with anger-management issues. For example:

  - Raising your voice, yelling
  - Confrontational body language
  - Talking over others
  - Pointing fingers or clenching fists
  - Threats and putdowns
  - Domestic violence, whether verbal or physical

- **Passive-aggressive behavior**: Covert (concealed or hidden) or overt (blatant) resistance to the boundaries or requests of others. Passive-aggressive individuals avoid direct confrontation by procrastinating, pouting, or misplacing important materials. Instead of communicating honestly about their thoughts or feelings, they show resentment and/or are obstructive in their behaviors. For example:

  - Claiming they agree, then complaining to others
  - Backstabbing
  - Doing only the minimum or making a halfhearted effort
  - Setting up others to fail (sabotaging)
  - Misplacing or not exchanging important materials
  - Not showing up on time or delaying a process
  - Partial responses

Recognizing unhealthy boundaries is the first step in forming healthy ones. Healthy boundaries not only improve the coparenting relationship, but they help you serve as a role model for your child's future understanding of healthy relationships. With healthy boundaries, you are aware of which emotions, thoughts, and feelings belong to and apply to you, and which belong to someone else, such as your child and/or coparent.

Examples of *unhealthy*, collapsed parenting and coparenting boundaries include:

- **The choice *not to*** say no to your child or new relationship when it is appropriate to do so, because you are afraid of rejection or abandonment.
- **The choice *not to*** stick with a plan; you change your mind depending on how you feel at the time or what others think of you.
- **The choice *not to*** set limits when others attempt to negatively affect your coparenting relationship.
- **The choice *not to*** remain consistent in your coparenting relationship because your identity consists of what you think others want you to be, so you change your actions and reactions to your coparent depending on who is around you.
- **The choice *not to*** maintain the balance of power or responsibility in your relationships, so you tend to be either 1) overly responsible for and controlling of your child and/or partners, or 2) passive and dependent in your relationship with your child and/or partners.
- **The choice *not to*** limit the sharing of problems within your coparenting relationship and your complaints about your coparent, meaning that you involve others, such as your child's teacher, your child's friend's parents, the coach, and so on.
- **The choice *not to*** limit abuse or to tolerate being treated with disrespect, including allowing others to treat your child or coparent abusively or disrespectfully.
- **The choice *not to*** rely on your own opinions, feelings, and ideas, thus creating inconsistencies in parenting and your coparenting relationship.
- **The choice *not to*** put the needs of your child above the needs of your intimate relationships.

- **The choice** *not to* have healthy relationships because you let your child run the show.

Examples of *unhealthy*, rigid (excluding domestic-violence circumstances) parenting and coparenting boundaries include:

- **The choice** *not to* say yes if the request involves interaction with your coparent.
- **The choice** *not to* be flexible and explore options with your coparent.
- **The choice** *not to* explore consistency and continuity in care between homes; instead, you rigidly insist on parenting your way in your house independent of your coparent's parenting style.
- **The choice** *not to* have contact with your coparent, so exchanges of your child occur with no contact between parents or at a public location, such as a shopping center or mall.
- **The choice** *not to* allow your child the maximum benefit of peer relationships and extracurricular activities during your parenting time.
- **The choice** *not to* allow your child the opportunity to spend time with or communicate with family members in the other household during your parenting time.
- **The choice** *not to* have empathy for your child or coparent.
- **The choice** *not to* actively parent, so you distance yourself from parenting responsibilities by either not spending time with your child, or having others such as stepparents, grandparents, or nannies take on your parenting and coparenting responsibilities.
- **The choice** *not to* consider that when you remarry you do not have a new family; you have instead added a new family member to your child's already existing family.
- **The choice** *not to* support your coparent and instead attempt to turn your child against your coparent.

- **The choice *not to*** ask for help from your coparent.
- **The choice *not to*** engage in authoritative parenting, and instead engage in rigid and punitive authoritarian parenting.
- **The choice *not to*** talk positively about your coparent to others.
- **The choice *not to*** have close relationships with the parents of your child's friends and to limit your child's time with them.
- **The choice *not to*** tell the whole truth, but instead tell partial truths or "spin" facts to create a false negative impression of your coparent.
- **The choice *not to*** engage in healthy respect and instead use negative-control techniques, such as sarcasm, shaming, name calling, retaliation, chronic lateness, jealousy, and self-victimization.
- **The choice *not to*** praise your coparent, but instead reinforce or support your coparent's self-limiting beliefs.

Examples of *healthy* parenting and coparenting boundaries include:

- **The choice *to*** separate your previous intimate relationship from your current coparenting relationship.
- **The choice *to*** share the decision-making for your child with your coparent.
- **The choice *to*** seek input from your coparent before making decisions for your child in most circumstances.
- **The choice *to*** respect your child's independent relationship with the other parent and other family members.
- **The choice *to*** recognize when the problem is yours or when it's your child's or coparent's.
- **The choice *to*** recognize whether your concern is really about your child versus yourself.
- **The choice *to*** be child-focused rather than adult-focused.

- **The choice *to*** ask for help from your coparent when you need it.
- **The choice *to*** terminate abuse or disrespect and be a role model for your child, independent of how your coparent acts.
- **The choice *to*** communicate your coparenting wants, needs, and requests to your coparent.
- **The choice *to*** recognize that you, not your child or your coparent, are responsible for your own happiness and fulfillment.
- **The choice *to*** seek intimate relationships with individuals who support your coparenting relationship.
- **The choice *to*** recognize your parenting and coparenting limits.
- **The choice *to*** allow your child and your coparent to define their limits.

Respecting your own boundaries involves asking yourself questions and being honest with yourself in several areas, such as:

- What is it you really believe? For example, do you "need" to be with someone because you are afraid to be alone and insecure, or do you "want" to be with someone because you love that person and you feel he or she is safe to be with?
- What are you capable of? For example, there is a difference between, "I can't sit in the same room with her," versus, "I am uncomfortable with her in the room, but I can do it because our child is important to me and my discomfort comes second to my child's."
- What are your true thoughts? Were you comfortable with the plans you made with your coparent, or were you okay with the plan until others said how bad the plan was and then you changed your mind?

If you would like to take a class regarding boundaries

and healthy boundary development, I offer an online course on boundaries at www.betweentwohomes.com.

Step 3: Understanding Feelings Versus Actions

"Between stimulus and response is the freedom to choose."
—Viktor Frankl

Understanding how the brain works is an important component of understanding how you as a human react to information you have just heard, seen, felt, or smelled. Deep within the brain's temporal lobes are the amygdalae, two small clusters of nuclei that are part of the limbic system. The central nuclei of the amygdalae are involved in the development of many emotional responses, including freezing (immobility), tachycardia (rapid heartbeat), increased respiration, and stress-hormone release.

When the stress hormone adrenaline is pumped into the bloodstream, it rapidly prepares the body for action in emergency situations. Thus, when you hear something you don't like, you may feel fear coming on, often masked as anger, and your amygdalae fire off adrenaline, creating an increased heart rate, flushed face, or a desire to attack. Your instinct may be to fight or to retreat. Lizards, fish, and other animals experience this same reaction when adrenaline is released.

Luckily, as humans, we have the prefrontal cortex. This brain region is used in planning complex mental behaviors, personality expression, decision-making, and moderating correct social behavior. The basic activity of this brain region is considered to be coordination of thoughts and actions in accordance with internal goals. The most typical functions carried out by the prefrontal cortex area are executive functions. Executive functions are the abilities to differentiate among conflicting thoughts; to determine good and bad, better and best, same and different, and the future consequences of current activities; to continue working toward a defined goal; to predict outcomes; to form expectations based on actions; and to maintain social "control" (the ability to suppress urges that, if not suppressed, could lead to emotionally unhealthy outcomes).

Ambrose Bierce wrote, "Speak when you are angry, and you will make the best speech you will ever regret." Often, "communication" is seen as occurring directly from our mouth to the ear of our coparenting partner. When parents are angry, they use excuses such as, "It just slipped out," or "They know how to push my buttons."

But true communication does not occur this way. You have to think before you speak. When you receive information, although your body may fire off adrenaline, you have the ability to regulate how you choose to respond. Your thoughts control what comes out of your mouth, and those words then go into your coparent's ear. Those words then go from your coparent's ear to his or her brain, and then he or she processes the information and chooses how to respond.

In other words, The Action (A) does not create The Consequence (C). Instead, Your Brain (B) regulates how you choose to respond to your coparent. The Action (A) occurs and then Your Brain (B) takes in the information, processes it, and allows you to determine The Consequence (C), or how you will chose to act. Thusly, A=B=C. The amygdalae may be shooting off that adrenaline, but the executive function in your brain can regulate this and help you think before you react. Whether you feel upset, sad, or angry, you can still control how you act. You are responsible for every word you choose to say and how you say what you say. *The only person responsible for how you choose to behave is you.* While you are not able to control how your coparent chooses to act, learning healthy ways to respond will likely reduce protracted conflict.

People often justify their actions by referencing their feelings. But, how you think influences how you feel. Changing your thinking can often change your feelings, actions, and reactions. For example, you may say, "I'm too afraid to perform a high-wire act in front of people." But, if you change your thinking to, "I know I'm good at this, and it's going to be great to hear the applause," it may help change your feeling of fear to one of excitement. Likewise, changing your thinking from "She's a bad wife," to "She's a good mother," will help you to work with your coparent.

Changing your thinking and asking yourself questions before jumping to conclusions can improve your coparenting communication. For example, Robin and Jamie are coparents raising their child Billy between two homes. Robin is twenty-five minutes late for the exchange of Billy. Jamie gets upset and thinks, "Robin does not care about my parenting time and can't be relied upon." Jamie then feels angry at Robin. Jamie sends a lengthy e-mail to Robin criticizing Robin's decision-making, irresponsibility, and "refusal" to stick with the clock. When Robin arrives with Billy, Jamie refuses to go the door to allow Robin to explain.

However, if Jamie was taking responsibility for Jamie's thoughts and actions, Jamie would act, instead of react, by exploring possibilities. In this same example, Robin is twenty-five minutes late for the exchange of Billy. Jamie is upset and thinks, "Robin does not care about my parenting time and can't be relied upon." Jamie then feels angry at Robin. However, Jamie then stops and questions the original conclusion about Robin's feelings and behavior: "Do I know that it's true?"

Jamie then thinks, "No, I don't know for certain that it's true. What are some other possibilities? Maybe Billy is sick, so they're running behind. Maybe Robin forgot the cell phone. Maybe Robin's broken down on the side of the road. I guess I could call to find out." Therefore, Jamie feels curiosity instead of feeling mad, discounted, hurt, or neglected.

So, Jamie calls Robin, who says, "I'm sorry, Jamie, I meant to be there by now, and I know I should have called, but I was rear-ended. I've been dealing with the police and my insurance company. Billy is fine; we're both just a little shaken up. I'm hoping to wrap this up in a few, and I'll be there as soon as I can. Or, actually, I'm not that far away if you want to come pick up Billy?"

If you feel like yelling or sending a nasty e-mail, you have the ability to stop, think about the possibilities and reassess your feelings, and then do.

1. Stop   2. Think   3. Do

How can you help the executive function remain in control? Imagine you call the other parent to offer him or her additional time with your child on Friday. The other parent starts yelling, "I wouldn't have less time with our son if you hadn't left me, you selfish jerk." Instead of yelling back and reminding him or her of the reasons you left, say, "Can you hang on a second?" and put your phone to the side. Breathe deeply, from your stomach; breathing from your chest won't relax you. Picture your breath coming up from your gut. Breathe in and say to yourself "calm." Now breathe in just a little bit more, and slowly breathe out saying "down." Get back on the phone and say, "Okay, you think I'm a selfish jerk, but would you like me to pick him up from school or will you?" Note that you allow your coparent to have his or her opinion of you, and by restating it using your coparent's words, you show that those words do not have power over you. You may have to do this more than once during the conversation.

Think about who has the power when you react to your coparent's inappropriate behaviors versus when you act and respond in the best interests of your child, no matter how your coparent is choosing to behave. Taking that deep breath may help you stay in control. It would be helpful for you to practice deep breathing when you are in a calm state, so you can use it when needed. Training such as this is just like physical training; the more you work out, the stronger and healthier you are.

Two books I recommend are *The Relaxation & Stress Reduction Workbook, Sixth Edition* by Martha Davis, Elizabeth Robbins Eshelman, and Matthew McKay for learning stress-reduction techniques, and *Feeling Good: The New Mood Therapy* by David D. Burns for more information about controlling your emotional reactions.

Step 4: Understanding Grief

In the family-law community, we have a saying: "In criminal law it's some of the worst folks looking their best, but in family law it's some of the best people looking their worst." How is it that great parents end up looking like victims in the courtroom? The emotional roller coaster of the separation process can be easily narrowed down to one word: *grief*.

The stages of grief are universal. Individuals experience grief in response to finding out they have a terminal illness, to the death of a loved one, to the loss of a job, and to the ending of a significant relationship. We have all been exposed to grief at some point in our lives. We have all had a pet die, or suffered through the breakup of a romance, or lost a friend. When these things happen, we experience intense emotions and do "crazy nutty" things in response to grief.

Generally, the grief process after the separation of a significant relationship is expected to last one to two years. The ending of an intimate relationship has been said to be second only to the death of a loved one in terms of its emotional toll. Not to make light of the death of a loved one, but when someone dies, they are dead. Couples with a child who they are actively coparenting experience the "death" of their intimate relationship, but still interact with each other on a regular basis. These couples experience many changes, from the dissolution of the relationship, to the addition of other family members when remarriage occurs. This continued interaction and change may prolong the stages of the grief process. While it would be nice if these stages were a checklist we could mark off, many individuals may skip a stage or likely regress to previous stages before they fully progress.

Elisabeth Kubler-Ross (1974) identified five stages of grief. The following is an example of those stages in comparison to a typical separation.

Leslie and Jordan have been married for eleven years and have two children. Leslie wakes up one morning at the first stage, where she is thinking about divorcing Jordan.

Shock and Denial – She does not want to think about leaving because it hurts, and she does not want to think about staying because it hurts. She talks to her religious leader, who tells her not to divorce. She talks to her family, who tell her, "Sweetie, we'll support you no matter what decision you make." She talks to her best friend, who tells her, "Girl, I wanted you to divorce him two years ago." She goes into "zombie mode," not really feeling anything.

In a couple of weeks, she moves to the second stage:

Anger – She now feels something, and it's anger. It must be all Jordan's fault that she wants to leave. So she looks for signs that they should divorce or sets little traps. For example, if he accomplishes a particular task, he loves her; if he does not do the task, he does not love her. Or she notices that the tree that they planted when they married is dying, so that must be a sign that the relationship is dying.

After six months or so, she moves to the third stage:

Bargaining – Leslie now regrets her anger over the past six months. Though the little voice inside her says the marriage is over, she convinces herself that if she will just work less, dress differently, or spend more time with him, the marriage will improve. So she goes through the motions of trying to make the marriage better and trying to "get those old feelings back."

After another six months, she moves to the fourth stage:

Depression – She does not want to think about leaving because she does not want to hurt the children, but she does not want to think about a future that involves living in this situation. So Leslie feels stuck, with feelings of suffocation, sadness, and hopelessness.

After another six months, she moves to the fifth stage:

Acceptance – Leslie accepts that the divorce will occur and it is time to tell Jordan.

So she walks into the living room and tells Jordan, "I want a divorce."

Where do you think Jordan is in the stages?

Shock and Denial, and generally within a very short period of time, Jordan moves to **Anger**.

Where is this couple right now emotionally when they

begin the process of separating? Jordan is stuck in **Anger**. Leslie is at **Acceptance**, wondering why he can't get over it (even though it took her one and a half years).

But it does not end there. In *Divorce and After: An Analysis of the Emotional and Social Problems of Divorce*, Paul Bohannan identified Six Stations of Divorce:

- **The Emotional Divorce** – End of the intimate relationship
- **The Legal Divorce** – Legal end of the marriage
- **The Economic Divorce** – Change in finances and financial independence
- **The Coparental Divorce** – Shift to two parents now single parenting between two homes
- **The Community Divorce** – Shift in family and friends and allegiances
- **The Psychic Divorce** – Shift from being married to single

Jordan is stuck in **Anger** as far as the emotional divorce, and Leslie is at **Acceptance**. Is this the best time to be evaluated by the court?

Where are they in regard to the legal divorce?

Jordan meets with the attorney and experiences:

Shock and Denial that it could take up to two years to finalize the divorce, quickly shifting to **Anger** because his new attorney tells him, "It could take less time if she gives you what you want."

Shock and Denial when Jordan finds out how much it costs as he is introduced to the word "retainer." He quickly moves to **Anger** because he is told "It could cost less if she just gives you what you want."

Shock and Denial because Jordan wants to have a hearing right away. He discovers there is "real time" and "court time," and court time is slower and more expensive. His attorney tells Jordan they will have a hearing right away, which in court time is six weeks away. Jordan then moves to **Anger** because he has to wait so long. He leaves his attorney's office in that same state.

When does Leslie get introduced to the litigation stages of grief? Generally when she is served by a process server giving her notice of an upcoming hearing where she has been sued for divorce and to pay Jordan's attorney fees. She then goes through the same emotions while meeting with her attorney when she finds out how long it could take, how expensive it could be, and how long before the first hearing. So now Leslie is at **Acceptance** in regard to the emotional divorce and Jordan is still at **Anger**, but both of them are at **Anger** in regard to the legal divorce. Leslie and Jordan begin to watch legal shows on TV, document journals against each other, and start preparing for battle in the courtroom.

A few days before the hearing, they become immersed in fear and panic, and have difficulty focusing on anything but the upcoming hearing. They walk into the courtroom at 9:00 a.m. Thursday and see that it's filled with people. They both think to themselves, "Thank goodness my hearing is at 9:00." They both experience **Shock and Denial** when they find out everybody there has a hearing at 9:00. They wait several hours before hearing their last name called by the bailiff. They stand up, their two attorneys stand up, and the bailiff says the judge would like to talk to the attorneys for "just a minute." But this is court time, not real time, and the attorneys disappear into a room with the judge for thirty minutes to two hours. They check on Leslie and Jordan occasionally, and then disappear again. Finally, the attorneys walk out with a *Temporary Order*. Now, both Leslie and Jordan are angry and feeling helpless. Is this a good time for them to be making critical decisions about their home, property, finances, and children?

You may relate to this story. You may have vacillated between these stages if you are separating or have separated. It may be time to assess where you are in the stages of grief and the stations of divorce, and where your coparent is. Using the following scale, rate yourself where you are with an X and where you think your coparent is with an O.

The fact my intimate relationship is ending or has ended

|————————————————————————————|

Shock   Acceptance

The actual legal divorce (the signing of documents)

|————————————————————————————|

Shock   Acceptance

Your future economic situation

|————————————————————————————|

Shock   Acceptance

Coparenting between two homes

|————————————————————————————|

Shock   Acceptance

You, your family's, and your mutual friends' adjustment to the separation

|————————————————————————————|

Shock   Acceptance

The fact I am about to be single

|————————————————————————————|

Shock   Acceptance

Over time, you may want to chart this again to assess progress.

If your situation is not one of domestic violence, child abuse, child neglect, or extreme conditions, then rather than duking it out in the courtroom and leaving it to a stranger with a black robe and a gavel to make the decisions for you, there are other options you may want to consider, such as mediation and collaborative law. (These options are explored in Chapter 4.)

In some cases, judges need to make decisions to protect the children and sometimes the adults. In my career while conducting custody evaluations, I felt very fortunate to have the opportunity to work in the legal system to protect family members from harm.

However, I also conducted many custody evaluations that did not warrant my work; in those cases, good parents were simply caught in the vortex of emotions stirred up by the grief process and were making poor choices at a very difficult time. It was clear to me that these folks were good parents yesterday and would be good parents in the future, but during their grief process, these adults shifted from being parents to litigants. Consider the impact of grief on your family and on the decisions that will affect you and your child's future.

Step 5: Taking Care of Yourself

"Don't let yesterday use up too much of today." – Cherokee proverb

Coparenting, as I have already mentioned, is difficult. During the divorce and separation period, children will often turn to their parents for support. Yet, when parents are going through a divorce, they often have the least attention to offer their children because they are struggling with their own feelings. Some tips to help you take care of yourself so that you have more to offer your child, include:

- Let the past be the past.
- Reflect on the past as an opportunity to grow.
- Look at this period as a time of growth and renewal.
- Maintain a good diet.
- Resume hobbies or start new ones.
- Take opportunities to have fun.
- Do not jump into a new relationship.
- Do spend time with positive people (not the "mouths" discussed in Chapter 3).
- Find emotionally healthy adults to vent to, and don't rely on your children to meet your emotional needs.
- Exercise.
- Take a hot bath occasionally.
- Take time out that is just your time to do what you want. Go to a movie, play golf, read, paint, garden, and so on. Treat this as your special time for rejuvenating.

- Get enough sleep.
- Monitor your emotions.
- Journal your progress.
- Remind yourself that if you are healthier, you are better able to care for your child.
- And most importantly, talk to a counselor if your emotions become too intense, or if you find yourself trying to drown your pain through food, alcohol, sex, or risky behaviors.

Step 6: Maintaining a Coparenting Alliance

There's a saying that addresses the power of the intimate relationship: "The opposite of love is not hate; it is indifference." When you love, hate, or are angry with someone, your emotions run very strong. When you are indifferent, you have very little, if any, emotional investment.

For coparenting to be successful, you need to make personal changes (how you think about and view your coparent) and behavioral changes (such as how you communicate with your coparent). The focus needs to be on your child versus your feelings and thoughts about your coparent. Professionals in the field of coparenting encourage the adults in both households to maintain a businesslike coparenting alliance.

The closer you are to someone emotionally, the harder it can be to separate your emotions from how you react to that person. For example, suppose you overhear someone call you a jerk:

- If it's someone on the street you don't know, the insult may not faze you at all.
- If it's a coworker you rarely interact with, you may feel uncomfortable sitting next to that person at a meeting, but your feelings probably won't decrease your ability to focus on work.
- If it's your good friend, you will take it very

personally. You may experience increased feelings of anger or hurt, you may have difficulty focusing when that person is around you, and you may want to confront him or her.

- If it's someone you are in an intimate relationship with, you will be affected even more intensely. You may feel betrayed, you may lose trust in him or her, and you may feel more insecure about the relationship.

I've worked with many couples who planned to remain friends after the separation, and on the surface that resolution worked just fine—until one or the other started dating. Some coparents are able to move to and maintain a friendly relationship from the start, but for many, it takes years of transition before they can evolve to a friendship-family type of relationship. The safest emotional place to be in a coparenting relationship is a businesslike relationship, especially initially.

When I use the example of a businesslike relationship, I am not describing two businesses competing against each other. Instead, I'm describing two employees working at the same level for the same company. These employees are not trying to one-up each other, but instead are working together for the best interests of the company. It does not matter whether the coworkers like each other, whether they respect each other (though they do treat each other with respect), or whether they like what their coworker does when he or she is off the clock. What matters is doing the job.

In a businesslike coparenting alliance, you are able to put your personal feelings to the side to work with your coparent to support your child. The foundation of the coparenting alliance mirrors several tenets of a good business relationship:

- **Dedication to the Product** – The product is your child's future, and it does not end at age eighteen. Your child is a never-ending assembly line.
- **Commitment to a Win-Win Relationship** – "Win-Win" means both homes working together to

achieve the overall goal: having an emotionally healthy, well-adjusted child.

- **Acceptance of New Ideas for Diversity** – Plans will need to change as your child grows. Seeking input from others may improve your coparenting plan. Added family members, such as stepparents, may provide new ideas that can enrich your child's life.

- **Common Courtesy** – Common courtesy not only improves your business relationship with the other parent, but also serves as a role model for your child. Courteous phrasing, such as "Please," "Thank you," or "I really appreciate that," promotes stability, goodwill, and cooperation in the coparenting alliance.

- **Communicating with Facts** – Don't stay stuck in emotionally charged positions and engaged in conflict, and don't regress to the past and past failures. Instead focus on current interests, what is accurate, and what needs to be done now and moving forward.

How do you get to and how do you maintain a coparenting alliance? First, you must remind yourself that your coparent will be your coparent for the rest of your child's life. Whether you like that person or not, no matter how mad or sad you are when you think about that person, the two of you are still a family raising your child between two homes. Therefore, you need to put your feelings to the side and focus on being mature, being responsible, and being a role model for your child.

Do not underestimate how difficult this can be. You may be curious about your coparent's personal life, and your coparent may be curious about yours, but unless those relationships affect your child, they may have to remain "none of your business" and vice versa.

Instead of seeing the situation as a failed relationship, see this coparenting alliance as an opportunity to start from scratch building a new type of relationship with each other. When issues arise, alert your coparent and plan structured meetings to address concerns by having an agenda and then sticking to the agenda. Putting specific and detailed agreements in writing will help ensure that the two of you are on the same page and that both of you have agreed to the same thing.

Step 7: Improving Communication

Words are some of the most powerful tools we have as humans. They have started wars and they have led to peaceful resolutions.

"But if thought corrupts language, language can also corrupt thought." —*George Orwell, 1984*

"Words! What power they hold. Once they have rooted in your psyche, it is difficult to escape them. Words can shape the future of a child and destroy the existence of an adult. Words are powerful. Be careful how you use them because once you have pronounced them, you cannot remove the scar they leave behind." —*Vashti Quiroz-Vega*

"Without knowing the force of words, it is impossible to know more." —*Confucius*

"Whatever words we utter should be chosen with care, for people will hear them and be influenced by them for good or ill." —*Buddha*

Family-Friendly Language

Words such as "possession," "custody," and "visitation" were never designed for parents, mental-health professionals, or educators. They were designed for judges and attorneys in a courtroom, and many states are even changing that. Legal professionals have been trained to use divisive terms throughout their education and practice, and unfortunately, parents, educators, and mental-health professionals have drawn their word usage from the legal profession. For example:

- "Fight for custody"
- "Custody battle"
- "Possession of your child"
- "Litigating the divorce"

The language used by individual parties, lawyers, and some mental-health professionals often promotes divisive and litigious conflict. The focus is on "termination" of the marriage, with only limited attention to restructuring the family. Misguided descriptions of the reconstituted family include terms such as "dysfunctional," "damaged," and "broken." For example:

- Children growing up between two homes are often stereotyped, as is their family of origin, with terms such as "broken" or "fractured" family.
- Terms such as "broken family," "your ex," and "visitation" do not promote shared parenting or the strength of the restructured family.
- Therapists ask children, "What is your visitation schedule?"
- Teachers ask parents, "Who has custody of the children?"

I have worked with many families where the parents have remained in the same home, and some of these families have done far more damage to their children and are far more dysfunctional than some of the families I have worked with who are raising children between two homes.

Rather than emphasizing the end of the intimate relationship, you should use language that emphasizes your family's strengths. Focus on the changes in the family system and the transition to a new way for your family to function. You and your coparent have the capacity to make your child's future an expression of human resiliency and regenerative potential.

Change your words, and you may change your child's

world and the potential in your coparenting relationship. The following are some family-friendly words to consider using; try to encourage the family and professionals in your life to use these words as well:

- Replace the word "visit" with "other home."
  For example, when talking to your child, say, "When you are in your other home" rather than, "When you visit your mother," or "When you are in your mom's home." If you are talking to someone else, instead of saying, "When they visit their father," say, "When they are in their other home with their father."

- Replace the word "custody" or "conservatorship" with "parenting."
  For example, instead of saying, "I have custody," or "We have joint," say, "We share the responsibility of parenting our child."

- Replace the word "possession" with "parenting time."
  For example, instead of saying, "It's my period of possession," say, "It's my parenting time."

- Replace the words "my ex" with "my coparent" or "father"/ "mother."
  For example, instead of saying, "I need to call my ex-husband," say, "I need to call my coparent," or "I need to call her father."

- Replace the words "custody arrangement" with the words "coparenting plan."
  For example, instead of saying, "Well, that's our custody arrangement," say, "We follow a coparenting plan."

- Replace the words "my child" with "our child."
  For example, instead of saying, "You need to take my son to the doctor," tell the other parent, "I think

our son needs to see a doctor. Can you take him, or do you want me to take him?"

"I" Statements

One great tool for improving communication is the use of "I" statements. When parents talk about issues related to their children, the parents' emotions are generally very powerful. Information that a parent might accept from a professional or neutral source is often rejected when presented by a coparent in a manner that feels like an attack. For example, if you start a conversation with, "You should have," or "You made me," you increase the likelihood of creating defensiveness in the other person. However, starting a sentence with "I feel" helps increase the likelihood that you will be heard in a nondefensive way.

For example, if I say to you, "You need to read this book now," you may become defensive, and you may not value what I say. However, if I say "I feel excited when I see you reading this book because it will help you improve your child's quality of life," you may be more likely to listen to me and feel positive about our conversation. Using "I" statements when you communicate verbally or in writing helps keep the coparenting relationship on a stable platform.

For many, the most difficult part of saying or writing an "I" statement is following the word "feel" with an actual feeling, rather than a thought. For example, "I *feel* you need to read this now" could be replaced with "I *think* you need to read this now," and it would still make sense. A feeling is an emotion, while a thought is a perception or an idea. Grammatically, "I *feel* excited when I see you reading this book" could not be replaced with "I *think* excited when I see you reading this book."

There are three parts to an "I" statement: 1) the feeling, 2) the specific situation, and 3) seeking a solution. An "I" statement is laid out in the following way:

I feel...
When...
Because...

Or

When...
I felt...
Because...

An expanded version of this for improved coparenting communication includes:

I feel...
When...
Because...
And it affects our child because...
What I do that may not help is...
The reason this does not help is...
What I would like us to do is...
If this is not acceptable, what are your suggestions?

Instructions for Completing an "I" Statement

I Feel...

- A one-word statement that identifies *your* feelings, not your child's or anyone else's feelings.
- This feeling should reflect what you saw or heard that led to this feeling.
- The words should reflect the degree of your feelings ("irritated" versus "annoyed" versus "angry").
- If you can substitute the word "think" in place of "feel" and the statement still makes sense, you need to reword the statement.

Incorrect Examples:

- Our child is hurt. (What do *you* feel? You can't speak for anyone else but you.)

- You are making the stepfather upset. (Again, this is about *your* feelings, not anyone else's.)
- I feel you don't care. (Does not describe a feeling; instead it imposes a judgment. Note that if you substitute the word "think" for the word "feel," the sentence still makes sense. Try "I feel ignored" instead.)

Correct Examples:

I feel:	Concerned	Disappointed	Excited
	Sad	Afraid	Happy
	Frustrated	Confused	Pleased
	Angry	Furious	Reassured
	Uneasy	Ignored	Comfortable
	Helpless	Offended	Appreciative

When...

You use the "when" portion to make a specific statement regarding what you have personally seen or heard.

- Use ten words or less.
- Keep it simple, clear, and precise.
- Use one "when" statement at a time, not a compilation of complaints.
- Don't express broad concerns; be specific.
- Use "our," not "my," when referring to your child.
- Avoid words such as "visitation," "possession," and "custody."
- Avoid broad criticism, such as "you always," "you never," "it's just like you," or "every time."

Incorrect Examples:

- When you refuse to talk to me. (Too broad. Need specific example; about what?)
- When you point your finger at me and won't call me

back. (One issue at a time.)
- When my son can't do extracurricular activities. (Use "our.")
- When you always make that expression. (Broad criticism.)

Correct Examples:

- When I requested the insurance card Saturday but did not receive it. (Specific incident.)
- When I did not hear back on Monday about Billy's medicine. (One issue at a time and specific.)
- When you told our son he couldn't play baseball. (The use of "our" and specific.)

Because...

- Used to explain the reason for your feelings.
- Brief (fifteen words or less).
- Your thoughts, not anyone else's.
- Use statements such as "*I* think," "*I* want," or "*I* believe."

Incorrect Examples:

- You don't care. (This is a judgmental statement that does not describe the reason for your feeling.)
- You should call me, not your mother. (Another judgmental statement.)
- You don't understand. (Another judgmental statement.)

Correct Examples:

- I don't think I have the information from you to help our child.
- I believe we need to communicate directly to role model for our child.
- I want us to be able to work together to raise Billy.

And it affects our child because...

- Be specific.
- Limit the portion after "because" to ten words.
- Make sure the portion after "because" starts with "he," "she," or "they." If the statement starts with "I," it is your personal issue, not your child's issue. Issues that do not directly affect your child do not need to be addressed in the coparenting relationship.

Incorrect Examples:

- You are not being a good role model. (This is a judgmental statement, and it is not specific.)
- I have to wait for you. (This statement describes your issue, not the child's.)
- I don't know what's going on. (Again, this is your issue, not the child's.)

Correct Examples:

- He does not get as much support from both of us.
- They are left waiting and can't do other things.
- She cries when she hears fighting.

What I do that may not help is...

- Do not be sarcastic.
- Briefly explain what you do that makes the situation worse or causes it to remain the same.
- Use this statement to self-reflect and take ownership of your own choices and actions.
- Keep it to fifteen words or less.
- Be specific.

Incorrect Examples:

- Let you get away with it. (Sarcastic.)
- I don't act appropriately. (Too vague.)

Correct Examples:

- Tell a lot of people about it.
- Argue during the exchange.
- Believe I am right without hearing your side.
- I say you "never" seem to care, but you care more frequently than you do not.
- I sometimes use the same curse word I am trying to stop you from using in front of Billy.
- I have been inflexible.

The reason this does not help is…

- Explain why what you do does not help the problem.
- Keep it brief, fifteen words or less.
- Do not repeat what the other parent is doing wrong.
- Use "I," "we," or "us," not "you."
- Don't use broad criticism; be specific.
- Use observations of the child's reaction, if appropriate.

Incorrect Examples:

- Because you continue showing up late anyway. (Repeating the complaint.)
- You don't make the situation better. (Use "we.")
- From 1993 until now, you have always put your needs first, such as when we were in Vegas, and you never… (Needs to be brief and specific, not broad.)

Correct Examples:

- Susie is still in limbo when 6:00 p.m. rolls around.
- We continue to argue in front of Billy.
- I involve other people in our situation.
- Our children's therapist recently stated that the children still feel caught in the middle.
- We both just get more defensive.

What I would like us to do is...

- Be very specific.
- Incorporate both what you can do and what your coparent can do.
- Keep it to twenty words or less.
- Avoid repeating complaints; stick to solutions.
- Use "us," "we," or "our," not "you."

Incorrect Examples:

- Get you to stop cursing in front of the children. (Repeating the complaint.)
- For you to show up on time. (That addresses what your coparent can do, but what about you?)
- Stop arguing. (Too broad.)

Correct Examples:

- Agree we both will not use the word &%$# in Billy's hearing range.
- Work better to be on time, be flexible when needed, and call each other as soon as we know we may be running late.
- To put our agreements in writing and not involve our parents and other relatives.

Full "I" Statement Example:

"**I felt** concerned **when** Billy had to wait twenty minutes past Friday's exchange time **because** I did not know what to tell him. **The waiting affects Billy because** it leaves him in limbo. **What I do that may not help is** I nag you even when you do call to say you may run late. **The reason this does not help is** that the nagging may decrease the likelihood of a call. **What I would like us to do is** call as soon as we know we may be running late so that Billy knows when to be ready. If this is not acceptable, what are your suggestions?"

Once you have agreed on a coparenting matter, you may want to put that agreement in writing to make sure you both have the same understanding of the agreement.

Increasing Your Chance of Being Heard

People listen best when:

- You give them your full attention, and you are willing to listen to them.
- You speak to them with respect.
- You do not accuse, blame, criticize, or put them down.
- You request, rather than demand.
- You keep your statements short and to the point unless they ask for more.
- They feel that you value their feelings and opinions.
- You ask for their help.
- You use humor from time to time.
- They think you have an open mind.
- You are willing to clarify your message.
- You don't use highly charged, exaggerated, emotion-laden words.
- You speak calmly.
- You spend more time in positive rather than negative interaction.
- The time is right!

Skillful Coparenting Communication

"Courage is what it takes to stand up and speak. Courage is also what it takes to sit down and listen." —Winston Churchill

- Ask permission. "Can we talk?" Timing is important.
- Speak in a pleasant tone of voice and avoid defensive body language, such as crossing your arms or putting your hands on your hips.
- State your ideas as your own thoughts and feelings, not as if they are the absolute truth.
- Don't try to read the other person's mind, make

assumptions about his or her thoughts or feelings, or expect the other person to read your mind.

- Ask for clarification, or rephrase what they just said to be sure you understand it. "So you're mad at me because... And you want..."
- Do not interrupt. Listen to the other person prior to expressing your own thoughts or forming an answer in your mind while they are talking.
- Separate a person's intention from their behavior.
- Never challenge the person, only the behavior.
- Stay in the present; don't bring up the past. In other words, focus on the current coparenting relationship, not the historical intimate relationship.
- Only discuss one coparenting issue at a time.
- Use "measured" rather than "brutal" honesty.
- Accept the other person's thoughts and feelings, even if they are different from yours. Agree to disagree.
- Put yourself in the other person's place.
- Be a good listener. Give the person eye contact if he or she is a visual learner, lean forward if the person is a hands-on learner, and use "I hear what you're saying" statements if the person is an auditory learner. You might want to vary your style until you find the one that works best.
- Don't expect a positive response immediately.
- Admit mistakes.
- Give information without insult. For example, "I'll be five minutes late," or "I'll make sure they pack that."
- Remove your "buttons." Use self-talk to stay in control of your feelings; don't let the feelings "control" you.

Guidelines for Effective E-mails Between Homes

1. In general, send only necessary e-mails and limit the amount per day.

2. Limit the topics to no more than three at a time, and fewer if possible. Each topic should be no more than two sentences in general.

3. Number the items to discuss so that when the other parent is writing back he or she can address the issues in the same format for easy response. Each number should be a separate item, not a continuation of the previous item.

4. Use your coparent's name to begin the e-mail, such as "Bill,…"

5. Use basic manners, such as "please" and "thank you."

6. Make your e-mail brief and specific. Only elaborate if the other parent requests more information, and even then limit your explanation to the information they are requesting.

7. Keep e-mails focused on the present or future.

8. Do not have others send your e-mails for you, and directly e-mail the person you want to communicate with instead of e-mailing one of his or her relatives or friends.

9. Make your e-mails nonjudgmental. Do not give directions on how the other parent should parent or coparent.

10. For the most part, keep the e-mails about appointments, activities, pick up/drop off details, and so on.

11. Give choices and be flexible when possible.

12. Ask instead of demand.

13. If you get an e-mail full of what you are doing wrong, don't take the bait. Respond as you would to a business partner or coworker. Focus on solutions.

14. If there are concerns, address them by using "I" statements. "I feel ... when ... and what I would like us to do is ...." For example, "I feel concerned when I see Bobby's low grades and what I would like us to do is to take him to a tutor. What do you think?"

15. When you receive an e-mail that asks for an

immediate response, let the sender know that you have read it. If you don't have an answer right then, let the other parent know when you will make your decision.

16. Don't speak for anyone else. You can say, "The children said..." or "I think they may feel...," but not "The children feel..."

Before you press the Send button, review this list. Ask yourself: Is this e-mail about the coparenting relationship, and does it meet all the criteria listed? If not, then stop and rewrite.

Step 8: Healthy Negotiation and Exploring Interests

"If war is the violent resolution of conflict, then peace is not the absence of conflict, but rather, the ability to resolve conflict without violence." —C.T. Lawrence Butler

Emotionally healthy families experience changes. Change is inevitable... except from vending machines. Children learn life lessons from watching how the adults in their life interact. They learn how to stay in school even if they don't like their teacher; they learn how to stay in a job even if they don't like their boss; and they learn how to communicate even when it is difficult.

Conflict is not always negative. In fact, conflict can be healthy when it is effectively managed. Healthy negotiation of disagreements can lead to:

- Growth and innovation.
- New ways of thinking.
- Additional parenting and coparenting options.

Einstein wrote, "In the middle of difficulty lies opportunity." As changes arise, work on finding the gray instead of both households seeing the situation as black or white. By exploring each other's interests, you may even find that black is the best solution, or you may develop a new option, such as blue. You may find sometimes that what you both want seems like the same thing, but it is actually very different.

There is a large difference between positions and real interests. Exploring each other's interests may help answer these questions: Why do you want what you want? Why does your coparent want what he or she wants?

For example, suppose a mother and father are arguing over who has their son on Wednesday evening. Both have the position that they need to have their parenting time with the child on Wednesday. They decided on a compromise: they would rotate the parenting time of their son to every other Wednesday. The father took their son to church every other Wednesday, because it was his interest for their son to participate in church as often as possible. The mother got to spend some Wednesday evenings with their son because it was her interest to spend as much time as possible with her son. Neither parent got as much as they would have liked, but given the situation, what else could they have done?

Better solutions probably seem obvious to you now:

- They could have agreed on another weekday night, which would have allowed the father to take their son to church every Wednesday and the mother to spend time with their son every week on another evening.
- They could have agreed for the mother to take their son to church every Wednesday during her parenting time.
- They could have explored if there were other options for additional church involvement.

But instead of exploring each other's interests, the parents focused on each other's position (the what): "I want him on Wednesday," and not on each other's interest (the why): "for him to participate in church" or "for me to spend more time with him."

42

People often confuse interests with positions. For example, a parent may be interested in fostering responsibility in his or her child. There are many possible ways of addressing this interest. One might be setting up chores for the child. Another option might be having the child take care of something, like a pet. Still another could be having the child organize a school folder for his or her homework. Focusing on interests, rather than on positions, makes it possible to come up with better agreements. Even when coparents have opposite positions, they have shared interests, such as raising an emotionally healthy child.

Families will have multiple interests, and it takes time and effort to identify them. To set the agenda for interests, parents can ask themselves questions, such as: What do we want for our child's future in terms of education, relationships, psychological functioning, and security with us as coparents? What will be important to our child in regard to these areas a year from now, five years from now, and when our child is an adult? Both coparents may not even be clear about their own interests in regard to their child. It helps to write down each coparent's interests as they are discovered and to ask why your coparent takes the positions or makes the decisions he or she does.

When developing optional solutions that meet the interests of both coparents, try to meet as many of each side's interests as possible. Start by inviting all sides to brainstorm ideas and write them down, no matter how crazy they may seem (before reaching a decision). Some obstacles to developing coparenting options are:

- Judging and rejecting prematurely.
- Starting by searching for a single best answer.
- Putting limits on scope or vision.
- Considering only your own interests.

To overcome these obstacles:

- View the situation through the eyes of your coparent.
- Focus on shared interests to make the process smoother for all involved.

43

- Don't reject any options at first.
- Hear the other parent out fully to understand their proposal.
- Look for meaningful opportunities, not simple solutions.
- Welcome diversity.

Only after both coparents have finished listing options should the options be discussed. Most people tend to immediately eliminate options before all options have been presented, which often limits the solution in some way. After all options are presented, determine together which ideas are best for satisfying various interests. Talk about likes or dislikes for each option. Explain why you like or dislike each one. You may hear something in the other parent's explanation that will generate yet another option to be considered. The options that each of you dislike can be eliminated. Consider the consequences for each one that remains. Those that both coparents agree upon become part of the solution.

For Example:

Jessie and Blake are separating. They need to come up with a plan for their son's education. Both parents agree that their overall interest five, ten, and fifteen years later is for their son to have a good educational experience and foundation for future education. Their next step is to plan how to get there, starting today. They begin to explore options.

Jessie wants their son to attend ABC private school, but Blake wants their son to attend XYZ public school down the street. Those are their "positions." So, what are their interests?

Blake asks, "Why do you want our son to attend ABC private school?"

Jessie says, "It's highly rated, the class size is smaller, and they have a great program to address his dyslexia. Why do you want him to attend XYZ public school?"

Blake answers, "That's where his siblings from my first marriage attend. With my back problem, driving two hours a day to ABC private school will be very difficult for me. XYZ is a highly rated public school, and I think it is an equally good education. And I can't afford to help pay for private school."

Now that both coparents have heard the "why" behind the interest, and not just the position, it is easier for them to develop options.

Here are a few examples of options that they could develop:

- Option 1 – Jessie could pay for ABC school and either drive their son every day or pay a driver to take their son on Blake's days.
- Option 2 – Their son could attend XYZ public school until middle school and then switch to ABC private school, or vice versa.
- Option 3 – Their son could attend public school, but they could hire a private tutor to work with their son on his dyslexia.

Example of evaluation of the options:

Jessie says, "I don't have time to drive our son on your days, but perhaps a carpool would be available or a combination of a carpool and a private driver could work. Would your back be okay if you had to drive it only one day a week? I could drive it three days, you could drive it one day, and I could hire a driver for one day a week, perhaps."

Blake says, "If our son could have a few years at the public elementary school that would allow him to make friends in the neighborhood, and his siblings would be older when he switches to private school. Hopefully, my back problem will be solved by then. How about if we enrolled him in public through fifth grade with a tutor for dyslexia and then switched to private school?"

As you can see from this example, the more that the parents talk about the things they like and don't like about the options, the more other options become apparent until eventually an acceptable option becomes apparent to everyone.

Once solutions are reached, put them in writing. This helps ensure that agreements are remembered and communicated clearly. Remember, each coparent must be confident that the other coparent (and any significant others) will carry out his or her parts of the agreement.

Step 9: Making It All About Your Child

When you run into a coparenting challenge, stop and remember why you are doing this difficult task. You are not doing this for the other parent; you are not doing this for you. You are doing this for the best interests of your child. You are planting the seeds for your child's future, and you are reducing the risks for your child.

"One hundred years from now, it will not matter what kind of car I drove, what kind of house I lived in, how much was in my bank account, nor what my clothes looked like. But the world may be a little better because I was important in the life of a child" — *Anonymous*

For your child:

- Maintain a coparenting-alliance relationship.
- Remember that a bad spouse does not equal a bad parent.
- Respect the autonomy of the other parent and the parent-child relationship.
- Stick with the clock whenever possible.
- Maintain flexibility, not rigidity.
- Keep each other informed and updated about your child.
- Maintain consistency.
- Live close to the other parent, if at all possible.
- Follow the rules for coparenting.
- Read books and visit websites that support coparenting.
- If necessary, use counseling and support groups.

Chapter 3: Obstacles to Coparenting

Obstacles to a successful coparenting relationship include:

- Domestic Violence
- Cognitive Distortions
- Litigation Thinking
- Shadows
- The Victim Mindset
- Pride
- New Relationships
- Special Topics

Obstacle 1: Domestic Violence

All the information contained in this book and any recommendations made to you should be considered in light of *whether you, your coparent, and your child are safe*. If you have realistic concerns about your safety in the presence of your child's other family members, some of the information in this book will not apply to you presently or possibly in the future. There is a huge difference between:

"I don't like being in the same room with you because I'm mad at you."

versus

"I don't feel safe being in the room with you because you have assaulted me."

While the best interests of your child usually involve better relations between the adults in both homes, it is never safe for you or your child to be exposed to domestic violence. Domestic violence will likely prohibit a fully successful coparenting relationship, and even if continued contact with the abusive parent is safe for the child, likely a parallel parenting structure will need to occur, with minimal interactions between the parents.

Domestic violence is the use of physical, emotional, verbal, or sexual abuse by one family member against another, with the intent of frightening, intimidating, and controlling the victim. Domestic violence also encompasses any threat that reasonably places a family member in fear of imminent death, bodily injury, assault, or sexual assault.

Not only does domestic violence occur while a relationship is active, the perpetrator of the abuse may attempt to continue the violence after the relationship has ended.

- **Physical abuse consists of:**
  Pushing, shoving, hitting, slapping, punching, biting, kicking, holding down, pinning against the wall, choking, throwing objects, breaking objects, punching walls, driving recklessly to scare, blocking exits, and using weapons.

- **Emotional and verbal abuse consist of:**
  Name calling, coercion, threats, criticizing, yelling, humiliating, isolating, economic abuse (controlling finances, preventing victim from working), threatening to harm humans or pets, threatening to withhold a child from a nonabusive parent, and stalking.

- **Sexual abuse consists of:**
  Unwanted touching, sexual name calling, false accusations of sexual infidelity, forced sex, forced pregnancy, covering up sexually transmitted diseases, and intentional HIV transmission.

The origins and dynamics of domestic violence are far more extensive than what I am presenting in this chapter. However, things you should know about domestic violence include:

- Alcohol and drugs *do not* cause abuse.
- It takes only *one* person to be violent.
- *Only the batterer*, not the person being abused, can *stop* the pattern of abuse in the relationship.
- Just because someone says he or she is sorry, and may even mean it at the time, that *does not* mean the physical or emotional abuse will stop.

Domestic violence has wide-ranging and sometimes long-term effects on victims and/or survivors. The effects can be both physical and psychological, and can affect the abused individual as well as any children who witness parental violence.

Children may develop behavioral or emotional difficulties after experiencing physical abuse in the context of domestic violence or after witnessing parental abuse. A child's responses to the violence may vary, from aggression to withdrawal to somatic complaints, such as body pain. In addition, children may develop symptoms of depression, anxiety, or post-traumatic stress disorder (PTSD).

Sadly, children who are exposed to domestic violence may repeat the behaviors of the batterer or the victim in their adult relationships.

Research indicates that partners who assaulted their spouse also frequently abused their children. Domestic violence is not limited to male perpetrators. There are women who abuse men and children, same-sex couples involved in domestic violence, and violence against the elderly.

If you are a survivor of domestic violence, get help!

Call the toll-free National Domestic Violence hotline:
1-800-799-SAFE (7233)
www.thehotline.org

**If you have committed domestic violence against a
significant other or your child, get help!**

Visit
www.stopvaw.org/batterers_intervention_programs.html

Obstacle 2: Cognitive Distortions

*"People are disturbed not by things, but by the view they take
of them." —Epictetus*

*"If human emotions largely result from thinking, then one
may appreciably control one's feelings by controlling one's
thoughts—or by changing the internalized sentences, or self-talk,
with which one largely created the feeling in the first place." —
Albert Ellis*

The way we self-talk and the way we talk to others has
a strong impact on our relationships. One way to improve
coparenting communication is to recognize and eliminate
common thinking and communication errors. Seven
common thinking pitfalls (cognitive distortions) that
coparents fall into are:

- Emotional Reasoning
- Imperative Thinking
- Personalization and Blaming
- Black and White Thinking (all-or-nothing, dichotomous)
- Extreme Thinking
- Mind Reading
- Ostrich Technique

Emotional Reasoning occurs when you create your
own reality based on how you feel instead of what the facts
reveal, or when you make decisions based on your feelings
without having all the facts. There may be many reasons
why someone does something, many meanings behind an
action, and many views of what actually occurred. Rather
than exploring the possibilities or examining all the facts,

you may be mentally stuck in one of these modes: "I feel it, therefore it is," or "Don't confuse me with the facts."

For example:

- "I feel overwhelmed and hopeless. Therefore, this coparenting situation must be impossible to solve."
- "I feel stressed; therefore, you're trying to intimidate me."

Example	Healthy Thinking
1. I feel nervous; you must be trying to intimidate me.	1. I feel uncomfortable dealing with you sometimes, but my feelings are my own responsibility, not yours.
2. You're just trying to make me angry.	2. I feel angry, but I am responsible for my emotions.
3. You're trying to threaten and terrorize me by discussing having our child do something that I don't approve of.	3. We have different philosophies about what is best for our child. Can we work to find some middle ground?

Imperative Thinking occurs when you apply an inflexible set of rules or beliefs about how the world is supposed to work. You have a set, fixed idea of how you or others should behave, and you overestimate how bad it is when these expectations are not met. Often these statements are expressed in the form of "I/you should..." or "I/you must..."

Examples include:

- **Entitlement Fallacy** – "I deserve it," "It's mine."
- **Fallacy of Change** – "You must change to suit me."

- **Fallacy of Fairness** – "It's just not fair, so you must make it fair."
- **Conditional Assumptions** – "If I do this, then you are supposed to do that."
- **Letting It Out Fallacy** – "It's bottled up, now I'm going to tell you like it is."

Example	Healthy Thinking
1. I have always been her caretaker in the past; I don't have to check in with you.	1. I use to be her primary caretaker, but now both of us are her primary caregivers in our own homes. We need to be on the same page.
2. You should feel/be concerned that she received an "F" on that paper.	2. I am concerned, but I realize it is only one paper and not her final grade, so I'll schedule a parent-teacher conference that you can attend if you'd like.
3. I *must* let her mother know about the appointment.	3. I *choose* to let her mother know because it would be better for our daughter if her mother was there to hear it from the professional.

Personalization and Blaming involves placing the responsibility for your actions or your behavior on your coparent or others. In other words, "I only did this because you did that" or "Well, you started it." You point the finger at others rather than at yourself and blame others for your choices and actions.

Examples include:

- **Faulty Justification** – "I'm late because you are never on time."
- **Rationalization** – "Why should I tell you our child's basketball schedule? You never come to his games anyway," or "Why should I tell you what the teacher said? You didn't bother to come to the parent-teacher conference."

Example	Healthy Thinking
1. I'm sure that comment was directed at me.	1. Actually, you never said that had anything to do with me; I just assumed it.
2. The reason we can't coparent is because you are totally unreasonable.	2. We are both contributing to the problem. I may be overreacting at times. Now let's learn better ways to hear each other and move forward.

Black and White Thinking involves all-or-nothing thinking (also referred to as dichotomous thinking), meaning something is either black or white; there is no middle ground or shades of gray. This type of thinking ignores any good or acceptable behavior of your coparent that contradicts your view of things and promotes a "my way or the highway" type of thinking. Black and white thinking ignores that there may be a variety of different beliefs or ways of looking at something.

Examples include:

- **Black or White Conditions** – "It's either good or bad," "You are right or wrong," or "It's simple; it's either black or white. There is no gray."

- **Name Calling** – "You are such a total jerk."
- **Destructive Labeling** – "You always" and "You never" or "You just don't care at all about her."

Example	Healthy Thinking
1. I can either call you as often as I want, or not at all. Which is it?	1. I can limit calls to important matters unless it's an emergency.
2. If you can't commit to taking him to every game we might as well not enroll him at all.	2. It won't be the end of the world if he misses a game or two, but can we agree to get him to all the games we can?
3. If you're not going to do it my way exactly, then fine, just forget it.	3. I see that something else is important to you; let's see if we can find some middle ground between what we both feel is important.

Extreme Thinking is a distortion in which the significance or extent of a behavior is exaggerated; in other words, making a mountain out of a molehill and blowing things out of proportion. It also involves giving little or no credit where credit is due.

Examples include:

- **Magnification** – "She feels devastated that you didn't let her watch that movie, and made her agree on a movie with her stepsister instead."
- **Minimization** – "Your showing up to that one play didn't mean anything to her since you don't show up for her other events," or "Just because you took a

day off from work to care for her doesn't make you father of the year."

Example	Healthy Thinking
1. You are never on time to pick up the children.	1. Actually, most of the time you are on time, but I'd like us to come up with a better plan for when you're going to run late.
2. You don't love the children because you don't call them daily like I do.	2. Parents have different parenting styles and find different things important in parenting.
3. You're trying to control my time with Billy by telling me about his friend's birthday party.	3. It's important that I support our son's peer relationships, and I appreciate your letting me know so I can decide to take him to the party or not.

Mind Reading is the belief that you know exactly what your coparent is thinking or what is occurring at the other household based on your assumptions. Rather than asking, "How do I know for certain this is correct?" an individual using mind reading will skip logic and jump to conclusions.

For example, a person may conclude that someone is reacting negatively toward him or her but doesn't actually bother to find out if that conclusion is correct. Another example is a person who anticipates that things will turn out badly and feels convinced that his or her prediction is already an established fact.

I sometimes hear from a parent, "I know exactly what they are like. I lived with them for ten years." To which I respond, "Oh, really, then why did you divorce them?" To which the parent responds, "Because they changed!"

Do you see the irony in the statement? You don't know exactly what is happening at the other home unless you are there, and you certainly cannot always know what someone else is thinking. People do evolve and grow over time, and the ending of an intimate relationship, later experiences, and increasing maturity can change someone's way of thinking.

Example	Healthy Thinking
1. I'll tell you exactly what you're thinking, because I lived with you.	1. We've both changed since the separation; please tell me what you're thinking.
2. If I do that, I know exactly what you'll do.	2. Now that we're focusing on the kids, how would you feel if I did that?
3. Billy will feel hurt if he can't go.	3. I'm not Billy, so I don't know how he'll feel. But I imagine Billy could feel disappointed. What do you think?
4. Your "new" wife just said that because she's jealous of me.	4. There are a number of reasons why your wife could have said that.

The **Ostrich Technique** involves thinking that if you ignore something, it will go away. Individuals who have low self-esteem, who have difficulty with multitasking, or who feel overwhelmed may ignore their responsibilities, often making the situation worse. They may ignore debts, which increases their late charges or interest rates. They may ignore their health, which leads to increased health concerns. They may not set limits with family or friends, which puts themself or their children at risk. In coparenting, they may not respond to their coparent's questions, which leaves their coparent and often their child in limbo.

Example	Healthy Thinking
1. If I ignore your requests for my half of the co-pay, you'll stop asking.	1. It's important for my son that I take care of my responsibilities, including the expenses for caring for him, so I'll provide a date when I will pay.
2. The children don't need me to finish the game; my boyfriend is calling.	2. My children are important, and if I leave the game, it sends the message that they're not as important to me. My boyfriend is an adult and can wait.
3. I live with my parents. I can't stop them if they say negative things about my child's other parent.	3. If my parents don't stop criticizing my coparent, I will need to move out to shield the children from their negativity.

Recognizing these distortions may help you not only communicate better, but improve your quality of life. Cognitive distortions interfere with your self-esteem, impair your ability to maximize your potential, and damage your relationships. If you are struggling in these areas, I encourage you to read *Feeling Good: The New Mood Therapy* by David D. Burns, and/or to see a therapist who specializes in cognitive-behavioral therapy. Your child is worth you making a change.

Obstacle 3: Litigation Thinking

"I am fighting for primary possession of my child."

Look at the sentence above and take some time to think about it. What words in that sentence tell you this parent has regressed into litigation thinking instead of seeking solutions for the coparenting relationship?

Let's examine the word "fighting." How could parents "fighting" over their child ever serve their child's best interests? Research has amply documented the negative impact that parental fighting has on children. Whether the parents live in the same household or states apart from each other, when parents fight, it's the child who pays the price.

Now look at the word "possession." When did your child become your possession? Your child is the person you love, protect, nourish, and encourage. Your child is a human being, not your possession. Now that your child has two households, it will greatly benefit your child if the adults in both households are involved in parenting and coparenting.

Sometimes parents blame their attorneys or what they have heard in the media for their use of words such as "possession," "custody," or "visitation." I ask them, "Do you go home to your children and say, 'Hi sweetie, the Petitioner's home' or 'the Respondent's home'?" Of course they don't, but in legal documents, parents are referred to as "petitioner," "movant," or "respondent," or in the case of a grandparent, an "intervener."

Another problematic legal word is "visitation." "Visitation" has historically been used as a legal term, though many countries have evolved into using words such as "parenting time" to describe the time a parent spends with their child. Unfortunately, family members and even some professionals started using "visitation" outside the courtroom. The word "visitation" applies to family members in jail, the cemetery, or the hospital, not to a child growing up between two homes.

When talking to or about your child, I encourage you to use sentences such as, "When you are in your other home," or "When he is with his other parent" instead of "visit." Encourage friends, family members, and professionals to do the same when they are in the hearing range of your child or assisting you in coparenting. In Chapter 2, I outline family-friendly language to use in place of litigation language. For example, "We are creating a solution to raise our child between two homes."

"I am fighting for primary possession of my child."

Please read that sentence again.

Whose child is this? When the other parent is in the room, or when you are talking to the other parent, the child is *"our"* child. Referring to a child who has two parents as "my" child indicates that you think of your child as a possession, but your child does not "belong" to you. Your child has two parents and benefits from the support and input of two emotionally healthy parents.

Many parents raising a child between two homes lose focus of this over time. Because a parent may hear only one side of their child's point of view, one or both parents may start to believe their child shares the truth only with that parent and not the child's other parent. The parents then argue over who understands their child better.

For example, the mother may say a child is afraid of roller coasters but is afraid to tell his father. The father may say the child loves roller coasters but is afraid to tell his mother. A professional interviews their son and asks the child his feelings about roller coasters. Most likely he will say, "I love them." So mark one up on dad's chalkboard. But when you ask the child what he loves about roller coasters, he will say, "They are scary." So both parents are right or both are wrong, depending on whether you see the glass as half full or half empty. Children often tell parents what they think their parents want to hear, and sometimes the truth they reveal is only a portion of the truth.

Many times, parents get so wrapped up in "my" child thinking that they give up the fate of their child to a group of strangers in an adversarial system.

It is *not* primarily the job of the court to make best-interest decisions for *your* child. That is the primary job of the family. Only when the family does not use better options are strangers such as judges, mental-health professionals, and others given the task of making best-interest decisions for your child. Does it really make sense for someone who will never know your child, never love your child, and never be there for your child's home runs or heartbreaks to decide your child's fate? Yet when emotions are high, it is easy for family members to become litigants.

"Your children have come into this world because of the two of you. Perhaps you two made lousy choices as to who you decided to be your child's other parent. If so, that is your problem and your fault." —Judge Michael Haas

These may seem like strong words, but whether it's a judge in Texas, California, Florida, or Minnesota, this tends to be the opinion of the family courts.

Parents in litigation often blame the court system. For biological or adoptive parents reading this book, there is only one person who is solely responsible for that other person being the parent to your child, and who is that? You may joke and say "tequila," but the answer is you. You made a promise to your child at the second of conception or adoption: "This is the parent I chose for you for the rest of your life." While you are not responsible for the behaviors of that other parent, you are responsible for bringing a child into the world with that parent or for securing that person legally as a parent.

For other readers of this book, somewhere along the line you may have made the choice to be involved in raising a child between two homes. And often one choice is to do the knee-jerk reaction of regressing to litigation thinking when there is conflict instead of seeking solutions.

In today's society, it is easy to litigate, and it's easy to get out of your responsibilities. You can swear before family, friends, and an official that you will stay with your spouse "Till death do you part," and then you can later file for divorce. Most states in the United States are no-fault states. If your debts get too high, you can file for bankruptcy. If you buy coffee at a restaurant and spill it on yourself, you can sue if you get burned. But for parents, the one commitment you cannot get out of is the promise you made to your children: "This is the parent I chose for you for the rest of your life." Litigation will not change that, though it might produce more conflict.

Unless you are protecting yourself or your child from valid domestic abuse, I challenge you to change your litigation thinking to solution-focused strategies to coordinate raising your child between two homes. I encourage you to work with professionals to help you keep your power within the family. In Chapter 4, I cover options to reduce litigation by using alternative dispute resolution.

Obstacle 4: Shadows

"Avoid drinking a big bucket of poison when you think you're going for a glass of ice water." —Judge Mary Sean O'Reilly

When you go through difficult times, such as divorce, separation, or a coparenting conflict, it is never easy to go through them alone. Unfortunately, during these times you are also vulnerable to advice that can cause increased concerns for you or your child. Behind each coparent lie the shadows.

So who are these shadows?

- Grandparents
- Stepparents
- Other family members
- Girlfriends/boyfriends
- Friends
- Internet websites and chat groups
- Support group members
  …and professionals

Most of the adults responsible for raising a child

between two homes know it can be very harmful to a child's self-esteem to hear one parent say negative things about the other. Though most parents start off believing they would never do this, some eventually make a negative comment when under stress or when frustrated.

Fortunately, sometimes a shadow is there to encourage them to stop and remind them why that is not a healthy behavior. Unfortunately, there are also relatives, friends, and significant others who encourage parents to engage in unhealthy parenting or coparenting behaviors.

You may have a shadow reading this book with you right now. Shadows can be emotionally healthy or unhealthy. I want you to surround yourself with "ears," and separate yourself from the "mouths" in your life.

"Ears" are the shadows who are family members, significant others, professionals, and friends who actively listen to your praises of and frustrations with your coparent or your child's other home. "Ears" are empathetic, but they do not tell you what to do or what to think. They respect your ability to make your own decisions. They may, however, encourage healthy behavior and constructive ways of thinking.

"Mouths," on the other hand, are the shadows who tell you what to do and encourage conflict with your coparent and your child's other household. They may possibly support you, but rarely do they support the best interests of your child. Their advice often justifies their own inadequacies and inability to regulate their own emotions. For example, just as alcoholics like to encourage others to drink, "mouths" will encourage others to think like they do and act like they do, and usually not in constructive or healthy ways.

If I am your "ear" friend, relative, or lover, when you complain to me about the other parent, how do I respond? I listen. I may say a few things such as "Oh, I'm sorry," or "That must be really frustrating," but I don't tell you what to do. However, I may encourage you to think of ways to improve the coparenting relationship or help you see other ways of thinking about the problem.

However, if I'm a "mouth," how am I going to

respond? I'm going to say, "Let me tell you what to do...," or "What you need to do is...." I'm going to keep you engaged in litigation by telling you to take my advice.

Online, you can find "Divorced dads hating moms" groups and "Divorced moms hating dads" groups. You will even find "step vs. bio" groups. Some of the most litigious coparents are the first to step up to tell other parents how to coparent and what they did in their litigation to "win." What they won't say is that their litigation cost over $80,000 and their child is still in therapy.

"Mouths" may become angry or disappointed in you if you don't take their advice. They may want to take over your role in parenting and/or coparenting, or they may use money to control your actions by threatening to cut off financial support if you do not take their advice. "Mouths" often want to control your actions. Jealousy, insecurity, a need to control, or other troublesome behaviors may lead a grandparent, stepparent, lover, or another relative to believe that he or she is a better decision maker than you when it comes to your coparenting relationship with the other household. "Mouths," by encouraging you to take their advice and by blaming the other home, often contribute to the victim mindset addressed in the next section.

From a child's perspective, the role of an emotionally healthy grandparent or stepparent is to be a grandparent or stepparent to the child first, before he or she is a parent or spouse to the child's mother or father. If two parents are fighting in front of their child during the exchange of the child—clearly an unhealthy behavior for a child to witness—what should "the shadow" do?

a.   Get into the argument supporting the person he or she is the shadow for.
b.   Remove the child if possible.
c.   Videotape the confrontation.
d.   Stay out of it completely.

The answer is B, remove the child if possible. "Ears"

will likely remove the child, while "mouths" will likely do A, B, and/or C.

The following table can help you ascertain whether you are dealing with an "ear" (a coparenting supporter) or a "mouth" (a coparenting detractor). Please feel free to take a picture or photocopy this table to hand out to your family members, friends, and even professionals who are involved in your coparenting relationship.

Coparenting Supporters	Coparenting Detractors
Do not involve your child in coparenting concerns	Bad-mouth the other household to the child or in the child's presence
Try to work with the other parent	Try to replace your duties or the other parent's
Assist you in working with the other home	Encourage you to fight
Trust you	Are insecure when you coparent
Encourage you to coparent	Encourage you to compete
Seek the opinion of both homes in coparenting decisions	Don't seek your opinion in decisions regarding your child
Recognize how important it is to reduce the distance between homes	Encourage distance between the homes
Encourage the children to have their own rooms with family memorabilia	Will not allow pictures of members of the other home
See themselves as part of your child's whole family	Focus on the "paternal" or "maternal" family
Help out if needed in the coparenting relationship	Intrude in coparenting relationship

Obstacle 5: The Victim Mindset

If asked "Who is the one person responsible for your

own behaviors?" hopefully you will say, "I am." And you'd be right.

Though most people are able to answer this question correctly, many still blame their actions on others, as described in Chapter 3 in the section about cognitive distortions. In court, these people may say, "The only reason I yelled, Your Honor, is because they yelled at me first." The reality is that people yell only because they choose to. When you are using the victim mindset, though, it is easier to blame your own actions on someone else by using phrases such as, "If you hadn't left me, I wouldn't be treating you this way."

When discussing the victim mindset, I am not addressing survivors of domestic violence. Instead, I am describing individuals who have trouble taking responsibility for their actions and instead blame their actions or reactions on others. Interestingly, batterers frequently have a victim mindset in that they blame others for their own actions with phrases such as, "Don't you make me do that."

Having a victim mindset not only decreases your ability to effectively coparent, but it is also not very beneficial in the courtroom, if you elect to litigate family matters rather than resolve them. One of the circumstances judges and evaluators are looking for is the parent who goes out of his or her way to share information with the other parent. For example, the judge may ask questions to determine which parent notifies the other parent well in advance of parent-teacher conferences and other professional appointments so the other parent may elect to participate. Those parents with a victim mindset blame their actions on others or focus on their own concerns. For example, a victim might say, "Well, Your Honor, I would tell him, but he won't come anyway," or "It would make me too uncomfortable for her to be at a meeting."

Examples of victim mindset statements include:

- "Well, she started it."
- "I just can't sit in the same room with that man."
- "I can't make my son go if he doesn't want to."

- "Don't you make me do that."
- "Fine, if all you're going to do is get upset, I just won't e-mail you about our daughter anymore."
- "The only reason I'm yelling at you is because you're yelling at me."
- "I can't help being this way; that's how I was raised."
- "I acted that way because you know how to push my buttons."

The following table compares victim mindset statements to responsible statements.

Victim View	Responsible View
He/she/they did this to me.	This dispute is an event that's happening to all of us.
The dispute is all his/her/their fault.	We all may be contributing to the dispute.
I never get a break.	I am where I am because of my choices.
Life is punishing me.	Life is a teacher, each experience is a lesson, and I am responsible for me.
I did it because he or she made me.	I am responsible for the decisions I've made and the action I've taken.
I need to be rescued.	I can take care of myself.
I can't.	I can, but I choose not to.

Because they have difficulty taking responsibility for their own actions, individuals with the victim mindset often seek rescuers. For example:

Seventeen-year-old Dana goes to work at the local grocery store and meets a coworker named Sam. Over time they become friends, and she begins complaining about her parents as teenagers often do. Initially, Sam responds with comments such as, "Oh, I'm sorry, that must be frustrating." However, as the months go by, the relationship continues to develop and they begin dating. Dana continues to complain about her parents, telling Sam, "Even though I'm seventeen, they don't want me dating, and they'd make me quit working here if they knew we were going out." Sam tells her he'd be willing to meet her parents, but Dana tells Sam that will just make things worse. Sam begins to feel very protective.

Sam stops being just a friend and becomes "the knight in shining armor." If Sam were Samantha instead, we would call her "Xena, the warrior princess." Victims and rescuers come in both genders. Sam now wants to help his girlfriend, to rescue her from her over-controlling parents.

One day, Dana says to Sam, "Oh no, I forgot to get a ride home."

He says, "No problem. I'll take you."

Even though Dana had already anticipated that answer, she says, "If my parents see me in the car with you, they'll figure out we're dating, and they'll make me quit."

"What would you like me to do?"

"How about you drop me off at the end of my street, and I'll just walk the rest of the way. I'll tell my parents a girlfriend gave me a ride home."

Sam hesitates. "Wouldn't that be lying to your parents?"

Dana bats her lashes and touches his arm. "You just don't understand what it's like to live with them."

Sam reassures her. "Well, I don't like lying, but if it makes things easier with your parents, I'll suck it up."

The victim/rescuer pattern has begun.

These two personality types attract each other. Rescuers often find their identity in helping others and are often attracted to people who need rescuing. From the rescuer's perspective, he or she is not in a relationship with an equal; instead, the relationship is with someone inferior and helpless who needs the rescuer to take control and provide protection.

The rescuer may feel a sense of self-esteem or status in this position, or enjoy having someone dependent upon him or her, thinking, "Here I come to save the day." In fact, when some couples go to marriage counseling and the individual with the victim mindset learns to take responsibility for his or her own actions, to take control of his or her life, and to become an equal partner in the relationship, the rescuer may want to end the relationship because he or she is no longer "needed" and will often then find another potential mate who needs rescuing.

Going back to the example, Dana eventually turns eighteen and wants to move out of her parents' home. She says to Sam, "I want to move out on my own, but I can't afford it. I could move in with a roommate, but what if I can't find a female roommate and have to move in with some strange guy? I just don't know what to do!"

Sam says, "Why don't you move in with me?"

Despite Dana having already thought of this, she says, "Oh, what a great idea!"

Sam and his gladiator friends go to Dana's parents' house to get her property. Can you guess when this usually occurs? If you guessed during the day when Dana's parents are at work, you're right. If you guessed at night, you must be thinking they're ninjas. They aren't.

Dana's parents come home asking, "Where's our daughter? Whose footprints are these? Where's her stuff, and where's some of our stuff?" Though Dana has attempted to hide that she was dating Sam, her parents figured this out long ago. Her parents call Sam, who of course has caller ID.

Sam tells Dana, "Your parents are calling."

"Oh, don't answer it. They're just calling to harass me."

Sam says, "Well, I'm not going to let them harass you," and turns his phone off.

Time passes, and Dana and Sam marry. Later, they conceive a child. Dana is now six months into the pregnancy and wants to see her parents. Sam protests, reminding her how terrible her parents are and how much stress they placed on her. He also reminds her that the OB/GYN recommended she reduce her stress now that she's in her third trimester.

Dana says she really wants to go, so Sam says, "Let's

just go together, and that way if things get out of hand, we can leave, and I'll be there for you."

"No, that will just make it worse. I want them to get to know how wonderful you are, but they'll think it's us against them, and I think I need to heal my relationship with them."

He asks her to think about it and to call her OB/GYN. Then Dana says, "You know, you're right. I'm not going to go."

Beautiful baby Bobby is born, and when he turns three months old, Dana wants to go to her parents so they can meet their grandbaby.

Sam is concerned, but says, "Let's go as a family."

Dana says, "No, that will just make it worse. I want them to get to know how wonderful you are, but they'll think it's us against them, and I think I need to heal my relationship with them."

You may already see the pattern of Dana wanting to keep Sam away from her parents ever since they first started dating. Individuals with the victim mindset often set up other possible "nests" before leaving one relationship or situation for another. They also like to keep the people in the nests apart. They will often exaggerate details, leave out significant facts, justify their own actions by blaming them on the person they are being rescued from, and tell the rescuer what they think will keep the rescuer on their side. They do not ever want these two camps to talk, because if they did, the truth would come out, such as how Dana's parents were not all that demanding and the details were exaggerated, or that Sam is really a very good person who is not as neglectful as she presented to her parents.

Dana eventually goes to see her parents, who are angry with her for leaving them out of her marriage and pregnancy. But as angry as they are, she says, "Mom and Dad, I should have listened to you and not moved out." She tells them how Sam encouraged her to move in, discouraged her from coming over to see them when she was pregnant, and is concerned about her coming over today.

While in Sam's mind, he is still the knight in shining

armor ready to rescue her at the drop of a hat, in her parents' minds, he is the spawn of Satan.

Dana's parents beg her to leave him, and a few years later Dana tells her parents, "You're right, Mom and Dad, I do need to leave him. I want to move out on my own, but I can't afford it. I could move in with a roommate, but what if I can't find a female roommate and have to move in with some strange guy? I just don't know what to do!"

Her father says, "Why don't you move back in with us? Just come back home."

Dana says, "Oh, what a great idea," as if she had not already thought of that. "But if I move in with you, I can't afford to pay you rent."

Her father says, "No problem, baby. You can just have your room back. You don't need to pay us anything."

"But what am I going to do about a babysitter if I have to work?"

Her mother says, "No problem, I can watch Bobby."

"But to get a divorce I have to have an attorney, and I can't afford an attorney."

Her father says, "No problem. We'll pay for your attorney. You can always pay us back later."

So whose behaviors are feeding whose? We see one person with the victim mindset and now three rescuers. Sam (the rescuer) "saved" Dana from her parents (the persecutors). Now, her parents (the rescuers) are "saving" Dana from Sam (the persecutor). Later, Dana will find a new boyfriend, and the cycle may continue. This pattern is called the Karpman Drama Triangle, coined by Stephen B. Karpman, M.D.

The Drama Triangle is clearly counterproductive to healthy parenting and coparenting. All of us have a bit of the rescuer in us, because it feels good to help others. All of us have a bit of the victim mindset in us, because it is easier to blame others than to take responsibility for our lives. But if this story resonates with you, and you see yourself in the role of the victim, the rescuer, and/or the persecutor, it is time to get off that ride and stop repeating the pattern.

An individual engaging in an affair may be a good example of the victim mindset, as he or she tells the spouse one thing and the lover another. In fact, if the spouse and the lover compared notes, they might be very upset with the individual with the victim mindset. It benefits the individual with the victim mindset to keep both camps upset with each other.

Other examples of how a person with the victim mindset sets up camps include the victim:

- Going to church in the morning complaining about the sinners, and in the evening hanging out with the sinners complaining about the people in church.
- Going to work and complaining about his or her spouse, then coming home to complain to the spouse about his or her coworkers. The victim refuses to attend company family picnics, claiming to the spouse that he or she doesn't want to give up family time to be with "them," and claiming to the coworkers that he or she would have come, but the spouse put too much pressure on him or her not to go.
- Telling a new lover how the coparent abused illegal substances and had an affair, but leaving out that he or she was the one who introduced the coparent to drugs in the first place and omitting his or her own substance use and affairs.

One of the first steps in breaking the Drama Triangle pattern is recognizing how it has played a part in your life. Once you are aware of your patterns, as well as the patterns of others, you can choose to recognize the warning signs and break free.

If you are the:

- **Rescuer** – Understand that many individuals with the victim mindset really do not want to take responsibility or may be incapable of doing so without intervention. They may act like they need your attention, time, love, support, money, energy, and nurturing only temporarily; however, the individual with the victim mindset will view this as a long-term contract and will turn on you when you are no longer honoring the contract.

You should also self-reflect. Rescuers often play the role of knight in shining armor or Xena, warrior princess, in an attempt to feel good about themselves, to gain attention or love, to feel more powerful, or to control others. They are often drawn to chaotic, dramatic relationships. The next time you feel drawn to an unhealthy relationship, think of protecting your child and role-modeling healthy relationships.

If your coparent remains stuck in the victim mindset, you cannot change that. What you can do is recognize the pattern and take responsibility for picking him or her to be your coparent.

When you meet your coparent's new lover, recognize that that person will be the new knight in shining armor or Xena, warrior princess, and the new rescuer will believe that he or she will have to protect your coparent from you. If you role-model healthy boundaries and respect toward your coparent and his or her significant other, it is possible you may find an ally over time, if the new rescuer becomes a stepparent.

- **Individual with the Victim Mindset** – Take time to self-reflect. Have you been manipulating different versions of a relationship story, depending on who you are telling it to?

Tell yourself, "Healthy relationships involve equals, both giving and taking," and "A role-model parent is emotionally healthy and independent." Be willing to be independent, to take responsibility for every aspect of your life, including your own happiness, finances, living situation, parenting, and coparenting.

Do not look to others to fix your problems. Recognize that by inviting others to take control of your life, you are inviting drama, which puts you and your child at risk.

Everyone can use help now and then, but before you ask for help or attempt to manipulate someone into helping you, ask yourself, "Is this a short-term request, and is there something I can do to give back during this time?"

Obstacle 6: Pride

"It was pride that changed angels into devils; it is humility that makes men as angels." —Saint Augustine

"Anger is the enemy of nonviolence and pride is a monster that swallows it up." —Gandhi

Pride is one of the biggest obstacles to a healthy coparenting relationship between parents and other family members. Samuel Butler wrote, "The truest characters of ignorance are vanity and pride and arrogance." Carl Jung penned, "Through pride we are ever deceiving ourselves. But deep down below the surface of the average conscience a still, small voice says to us, something is out of tune."

From the previous section, do you think Sam (the rescuer, now persecutor) wants to admit that he was that gullible and naïve since day one when he met Dana, and that Dana's parents are actually good people? No, due to his pride, he would rather believe their marriage was just fine until her parents got involved, moved her away from him, and financed her divorce from him.

Do you think Dana's parents (the persecutors now rescuers) who begged her to leave her husband, who let her live with them rent free, who babysat for free, and who paid for her attorney want to admit Sam is a good guy? No, due to their pride, they would rather believe the reason she continues to be burdened and make poor choices in relationships is because of Sam and her experiences with him.

Pride can cloud the mind and interfere with your ability to see the reality of situations. Because pride is self-focused, it is easy to ignore the needs of your child when your thoughts are distorted and your amygdalae are firing off adrenaline.

Let's say your child is out on the soccer field sweating up a storm. The coach calls a break, and you reach into the cooler to pull out a bottle of water for your child. On the other side of the cooler, your coparent arrives with his or her new girlfriend or boyfriend. How should you respond?

No, the answer is not, "The water bottle becomes a projectile."

When you meet the new girlfriend or boyfriend, reach out your hand and say "Hi, I'm _____."

Why do this? Hopefully, you got the answer right...

"For your child."

If you instead start an argument or just ignore that person, your behavior will put your child in a very difficult, uncomfortable, and embarrassing situation. Five years later, your child might not even remember that other person, but your child will remember how embarrassing your behavior was at the soccer game.

By feeling one way but putting your pride aside and acting differently, you protect your child from your unhealthy emotions. You role model for your child healthy interactions and send the message, "You are important to me."

Obstacle 7: New Relationships

When should you introduce your child to a new significant other? I recommend you don't if you are still married. Bringing new relationships into the picture too quickly can negatively affect the coparenting relationship and put emotional strain on your child. Going through a divorce is a transitional period for both parents, as well as your child, and new relationships can introduce a new set of problems.

Prior to separation, your child relies on you not only as a parent but also sees you and your coparent as a couple and a united front: "my parents." Once both parents separate, your child will benefit from having time to form an attached relationship with just you single parenting them when he or she is with you in your home.

One concern of exposing your child to a new relationship before you are divorced is that you are teaching him or her that it is okay to have affairs, which may not be a precedent you want to set for your child's future. By jumping quickly into a new relationship, you may teach your child that he or she *needs* to be in a relationship at all times. This lesson may increase the child's likelihood of becoming codependent and may encourage him or her to jump between relationships, instead of learning how to be independent and take time to heal between relationships.

It is understandable that after a separation, you may feel lonely or desire the company of someone you find attractive. However, if you bring a significant other into your relationship with your child too soon, you may be giving your child the message that he or she is not your priority. Most children need individual attention to help them adjust to transitions such as separation, having two homes, and divorce. Your desire to get immediately involved in another relationship may signal to your child that his or her needs are not that important to you.

Many children have reconciliation fantasies and hope that someday there will be one home instead of two, with both parents living together again. Seeing one of his or her parents dating soon after the separation can be very confusing and frustrating to a child.

One of the biggest complaints parents have after a separation is how little time they spend with their child. Most of us did not have a child so that the child could spend almost half of his or her life growing up in another home. A better time to be involved in intimate relationships is when you are not with your child, rather than during your parenting time. In other words, if you see your child on the first, third, and fifth weekends of a month, then if you choose to date, do so on the second and fourth weekends, or on days of the week that do not involve your parenting time.

Remember, you are one of the role models for your child's future relationships. During the divorce and for several months following the divorce is a time to focus on healing yourself, distancing yourself from codependent behaviors, and meeting the needs of your child during the time your child is with you.

You may think it is time to move on, but think about your child, who is not in the same place you are. Remember the stages of grief? Your child experiences them too, but somewhat differently than you do. How children experience and react to grief is discussed in Part 2, Chapter 6, and it's important to understand what's happening to your child during this process.

Your child's family and living circumstances are changing dramatically. It takes time for your child to adjust, to heal, and to feel secure in his or her new living circumstances. Your child needs you to role model that you are capable of single parenting alone. Your child also needs you to help him or her let go of any dreams of having both coparents in one home again. You can teach your child:

- That you are a capable parent who can care for him or her without needing to have a lover by your side during this transitional period.
- To be independent rather than codependent.
- That love takes time, healing, and patience. That listening to your head is more important than listening to your heart or the rush of your hormones.

You may ask: How long should I wait before introducing or reintroducing my children to a new relationship post-divorce?

a. Right away to see how your lover responds to your

child and how your child responds to him or her.
b.   After three to six months of actively dating.
c.   Depends on the situation.
d.   After you have asked your child if it's okay.

The correct answer is B. I recommended that you actively date at least three to six months prior to exposing or reintroducing your child to a new relationship. Active dating is *not* chatting on the Internet or talking on the phone; it is being physically in the presence of that person on a regular, ongoing basis so that you can closely observe and truly get to know that person. Anyone can appear wonderful online or on the phone or even pretend to be someone that they're not.

So why wait? At one extreme, suppose the person is great with children and your child grows attached to that person and/or his or her children. Unfortunately, you didn't take the time to get to know that person well, and the relationship soon ends. Now your child has just lost someone else he or she cares about right after going through the pain of a divorce.

At the other extreme, suppose the person you want to introduce to your child is a pedophile, a batterer, or has other serious problems that he or she is able to mask temporarily. Unacceptable traits typically don't come to light during the first three months of dating because everyone is on his or her best behavior.

Consider three reasons a person might want to meet your child too quickly:

- He or she wants to abuse your child and you look like you might allow that to happen.
- He or she wants to use your child to win you over.
- He or she doesn't have malicious intentions, but doesn't understand how quickly your child can become attached and doesn't understand the impact it will have on your child if the relationship falls apart.

It's always in the best interests of your child to not

introduce someone new until you have thoroughly vetted that person and are certain that the relationship will be a lasting and healthy one.

After the divorce is finalized, you may meet the right person not only for you, but for your child. A new relationship does not have to be an obstacle to the coparenting relationship. Stepfamily members can be wonderful, supportive additions to the family.

Your child can never have too many emotionally healthy people who love him or her, and a stepparent, stepgrandparents, and stepsiblings can be a huge bonus to the family. Stepparents can be an asset to the home and the coparenting relationship.

If you and your significant other focus on your child's interests, a stepfamily can present great opportunities. However, realize that if you choose to remarry or share a home with someone, you are not creating a new family. You are instead adding to your child's already existing family. The core family for your child is his or her parents, and anyone else who comes along can either be a great extension to the family or can create more chaos and conflict.

Bottom line: Look for someone who not only meets your needs, but who also complements your child's already existing family.

Unfortunately, new relationships and stepparents can sometimes be a huge obstacle to the coparenting relationship and to your child's best interests. Be alert to new relationships or stepparents who encourage dividing the maternal and paternal parts of a child's family, and recall the previous sections regarding "ears" and "mouths," the coparenting supporters and coparenting detractors.

If you are selective, you will find relationships and even possibly a stepparent who values your relationship with your coparent, values your child, and does not want to replace your role or the other parent's role. Such a person will be secure enough in his or her relationship with you to encourage you to work directly with your coparent and will see himself or herself as part of the team in helping the coparenting relationship thrive.

There are plenty of fish in the sea, but once you have a child and are coparenting, you need to be careful where you cast your net and extra choosy when deciding which fish to keep and which to toss back.

Obstacle 8: Special Topics

Substance Abuse

It is important for children to be safe when under the care of a parent. Abuse of alcohol, illegal drugs, or prescription medication impairs a parent's ability to make timely and appropriate decisions during his or her parenting time, regulate his or her emotions (Barnard and McKeganey 2004), and effectively coparent with the other home.

If substance abuse is an issue for one of the coparents, a parallel parenting arrangement may serve the children better. If a case goes to trial, the court may order supervised parenting time, or other safety measures may be put in place to protect children from witnessing substance abuse or suffering from the impaired parenting of a parent under the influence.

Substance abuse may prohibit a successful coparenting relationship. It is important that the parent abusing substances get help and that his or her coparent understand the complex issues related to substance abuse.

The following links may be helpful:

www.findtreatment.samhsa.gov
www.helpguide.org/topics/addiction.htm

Mental Illness

Mental illness takes many forms, affects individuals differently, and appears in various degrees of severity. However, a severely mentally ill parent places a child at risk of abuse, neglect, and developmental delay. According to Gregoire and Manning (2009), these parents may, "Affect attachment formation and the cognitive, emotional, social, and behavioral development of children. These children are also at increased risk of developing psychiatric disorders in childhood, adolescence, and later adult life."

Mental illness may make having an emotionally healthy, cooperative coparenting relationship impossible, and a parallel parenting arrangement may serve the children better. As with substance abuse, if a case goes to trial, the court may order supervised parenting time or other safety measures may be put in place to protect the children.

Severe mental illness may prohibit a successful coparenting relationship. It is important that the parent with mental-health concerns gets help and that his or her coparent understands the complex issues related to mental illness.

The following links may be helpful:

www.nami.org
www.nimh.nih.gov/health/find-help/index.shtml
www.findtreatment.samhsa.gov
www.samhsa.gov/MentalHealth/TraumaticEvent.aspx
www.suicidepreventionlifeline.org/GetHelp

If your coparent suffers from narcissistic, histrionic, high conflict, or borderline traits, I also recommend the books *Splitting: Protecting Yourself While Divorcing Someone with Borderline or Narcissistic Personality Disorder* by Bill Eddy and Randi Kreger and *BIFF: Quick Responses to High Conflict People, Their Personal Attacks, Hostile Email and Social Media Meltdowns* by Bill Eddy.

Military Families

When one or both coparents are in the military and deployed away from their child, it creates complications in the coparenting relationship. The military may not allow the flexibility of a schedule or even the possibility of following the court order or a mutually agreed upon parenting schedule. Shared decisions may be more complicated, and other family members of the parent in the military may be granted more access to your child.

It is important that:

- The parent that is away have frequent contact with your child.
- Both homes still work together as much as possible, even if the role of one parent is temporarily replaced by another relative.
- If possible, that you develop a coparenting plan prior to deployment.

The following links may be helpful:

www.focusproject.org/home
www.realwarriors.net/family/children/deployment.php
www.sesamestreet.org/parents/apps (see "Family Tool Kits")
www.skype.com
www.uso.org/programs/military-families/
www.samhsa.gov/MilitaryFamilies/
www.veteranscrisisline.net/

Chapter 4: Legal Matters

(If the legal matters regarding your child have been finalized, you may want to skip Chapter 4.)

- Legal Terms and Knowing Your State Laws
- Alternatives to Litigation
- Obstacles to Alternative Dispute Resolution

Legal Terms and Knowing Your State Laws

I am not an attorney, so please consider that the following information is based on my understanding of family-law terms. It is important that you know the laws in your state regarding family-law matters, and the best resource is likely your attorney. Laws change, so it is important that you find current information.

What are the forms of custody, and the differences between them?

- Sole Managing Conservatorship (Custody) – Generally, this means one parent has most, if not all, of the rights, duties, and privileges to make decisions for the child. The other parent will likely have very limited rights or even minimal access to the child.
- Joint Managing Conservatorship (Custody) – This does not necessarily mean fifty-fifty time share or rights, though in some cases it does. There are two components to this:

  - *Legal decision-making* regarding the upbringing of the child, such as educational, extracurricular, medical, therapeutic, and religious decisions.
  - *Physical care* of the child during a parent's parenting time, which includes supervision of the child.

Other terms to be familiar with:

- Ad Litem – In some cases, an attorney for the child is appointed. This attorney is referred to generally as the Ad Litem, Guardian Ad Litem, or Amicus Attorney. The title and responsibilities of this role vary from state to state.
- Access, Visitation, Period of Possession, or Parenting Time – Terms found in court orders regarding the child's time with either parent.
- Alternative Dispute Resolution – Options available to resolve legal matters without involving the court.
- Court Order – A written order signed by a judge that the adults are required to follow. This order may be produced by agreement or at the sole discretion of a judge.
- Exchange – The transfer of a child between each parent's parenting time.
- Hearing – Appearance of the parents and their attorneys before the judge.
- Maternity – Legal establishment of the mother of a child.
- Modifications – Motions filed after the final decree, or basically returning to court. Child support and parenting-time schedules are typical issues involved in modifications.
- Parenting Plan – A document created by a judge or by agreement of the family that details the schedule between homes and the rights, duties, and privileges of each parent.
- Paternity – Legal establishment of the father of a child.
- Primary Residence – The residence of the child for the purpose of public school enrollment and/or where the child may spend more time.
- Pro Se – A litigant without legal representation.
- Supervised visits or exchanges – The parenting time of a parent, or the exchange between the parents, is supervised by an individual or entity.

- Trial – A formal hearing in which the parents and attorneys are present in addition to witnesses and the presentation of evidence.

Considering a Lawyer?

In *Considering Divorce? Critical Things You Need To Know* by Melinda Eitzen, Joanna Jadlow, and Brenda Lee Roberts, Eitzen suggests you consider the following:

- "Is the lawyer's practice primarily focused on family law? The law changes continuously. A lawyer who focuses their practice in one area is more likely to be up to speed on recent changes in the law, the preferences of the judges, the current practices in each court, and the alternative dispute resolution processes such as collaborative, mediation and arbitration.
- Is the lawyer well regarded by his or her peers? Lawyers see each other's work product every day when we have cases together. We see each other's written work product and performance in the Courtroom and in collaborative meetings. Lawyers know better than anyone who is ethical and who is not. Who is smart and hardworking, and who is not. One way to find this out is to call a few divorce lawyers and ask them who the top three lawyers are that they would hire besides themselves and their firm.
- Has the lawyer been in trouble with the state bar association? In Texas, you would go to www.texasbar.com and enter the lawyer's name to see if he or she has been the recipient of any public sanctions or disciplinary action.
- Spend the time and money to interview two to three lawyers. Family law is very personal and you should feel comfortable with the lawyer you decide to hire. Observe how responsive the lawyer and their staff are during this initial contact. The number one

complaint against lawyers is the failure to call their clients back in a timely manner. How the lawyer handles your initial contact could give you an indication of whether or not that lawyer and their firm are prompt in their attentiveness to client needs.

- Ask the lawyers you interview various questions, such as: What percentage of your practice is family law? What is likely to be their approach to your case based on the facts you have given them? Do they practice in both collaborative and litigation models? Do they feel more comfortable in collaborative or litigated cases?"

For the bar association in your state, go to:

www.americanbar.org/groups/bar_services/resources
(follow the link under Bar Association Directories)

Alternatives to Litigation

When you need to resolve family-law matters, one obvious option is to litigate them. But did you know there are other options besides fighting in court?

No matter what circumstance created the situation where legal resolution must be achieved for children growing up between two homes, there are options that allow families to resolve the situation in confidential and nonadversarial settings. These options are called alternative dispute-resolution services.

The most common complaint I have received at the end of my live or online coparenting class is that parents wish they had received this information earlier in the process. They report that they were not made aware of alternative-dispute options. So what are those options?

- *Kitchen Table Approach* – This method involves direct negotiation between family members without professional involvement. The family may design its own coparenting plan. This works well if the family members are at a high-functioning point in their lives and can effectively communicate with each other. The family members reach agreements and draw up these agreements in a document. One parent then takes this document to an attorney who creates a legal document, which that parent submits to the court. In some cases, the family members may be able to draw up the legal documents themselves, but they risk the lack of legal advice that could negatively impact either coparent or their child in the future.

- *Cooperative Parenting* – Sometimes families reach impasses that prevent them from resolving coparenting challenges. Cooperative parenting is a confidential process where families can meet with a licensed mental-health professional who is trained in mediation and coparenting matters to develop a written parenting plan. With the help of the professional, the parents develop a coparenting plan that outlines current and future details regarding how the coparents will raise their child between two homes. If the plan involves legal matters, the family members then take this document to their attorneys to seek input and convert the plan to a legal document.

- *Collaborative Law* – A confidential process in which both parties retain separate lawyers whose primary role in advocating for their client is to help the parents resolve issues. The parents and their lawyers sign a collaborative-law participation agreement, in which they agree to communicate respectfully and be cooperative in providing information needed for resolution. The attorneys also agree to withdraw if one party is not operating in good faith or if one or both parents decide to litigate. This approach often includes allied specialists, such as a communications facilitator, a financial planner, and a child specialist, who work with the family to create a successful plan.

To find collaborative-law professionals in your area, go to collaborativepractice.com.

- *Early Intervention Mediation* – A confidential process where the family members work together with a trained neutral mediator or mediators to craft a plan. This process typically, though not always, occurs prior to hiring attorneys. This method is often used before a divorce is filed or at the onset of filing. The mediator meets with the parties in joint sessions where the mediator assists each party in communicating his or her interests and needs to each other, facilitates negotiations between the parties, and drafts a written agreement. Between sessions, the parties may consult with their attorneys, if any, a coparenting specialist, and/or a financial planner. At the end of the process, a settlement agreement is prepared. The parties then either file Pro Se or each hire an attorney, if they have not already, to prepare the necessary court documents to finalize the uncontested legal matter.

  For more information, go to www.mediate.com.

- *Mediation* – Mediation is a confidential process conducted by a trained, impartial third party (the mediator) whose role is to assist two (or more) parties to a dispute in reaching an agreement. Attorneys for both parents are typically present during sessions. Mediation may occur with 1) both parents in the same room at all times, 2) both parents separated at all times in a "caucus" format, or 3) a combination of these options. In some cases, when the parents cannot reach an agreement about issues they are attempting to mediate, the matter may be arbitrated, which is another alternative, but is less commonly used in family-law matters. Arbitration similarly involves a trained, impartial third party (the arbitrator) who listens to each party's case and makes decisions about any contested issues, similar to a judge, but in a much less formal atmosphere. In some states, arbitration is binding on the parties only if they have agreed in writing to be bound by the result.

For more information, go to www.mediate.com.

- *Parenting Coordination* – Even when the coparents are experiencing a high level of conflict, options other than litigation exist. Parenting coordination is typically court ordered as a child-focused alternative dispute-resolution process, in which a specialized professional (a parenting coordinator) with mediation training and experience assists the parents in resolving their disputes and educating the parents about their children's needs. In some states, with prior approval of the parties and/or the court, the parenting coordinator may make decisions within the scope of the court order or appointment contract if the parents are unable to agree on their parenting plan. The process may or may not be confidential, depending on your state and your state's laws.

For more information about parenting coordination, go to parentingcoordinationcentral.com.

Obstacles to Alternative Dispute Resolution

- **"My" Child Mindset** – As I covered in Chapter 3, when you are in the mediation session with the other parent, refer to "our" child or "our" children.

- **Distance Between Homes** – As Judge Terri White says, "It's really hard on children to have a relationship first of all with the parent that they do not live close to. Yes they can e-mail, yes they can talk on the phone, yes they may be able to see that parent once a month and on holidays, but that is not the same as having your parent interact in your life on a daily or weekly basis with you and your activities."

The greater the distance between two homes, the greater the difficulties for the child. If your child has to travel a great way between homes, your child will be less able to take full advantage of having two homes and will experience more interference in his or her peer relationships and extracurricular activities. If you are considering moving away from your coparent, take the time to review the article "My Long-Distance Life" by Nick Sheff, located at akidsright.org/newsweek.htm. Research (Fabricius and Braver, 2006) indicates that long distances between homes create the following problems for children:

o More inner turmoil and distress about the parental divorce
o Worse relationship with nonresident parents
o Worse relationship between the parents

However, if there will be a great distance between you and your child, there are some good resources available to help you stay in touch, such as live video conferencing, and you can include these tools in your coparenting agreement. The term "virtual parenting time" has been coined by a growing number of courts and parents. You may want to purchase the book *101 Ways to Be a Long-Distance Super-Dad... or Mom, Too!* by George Newman. For more information about online tools, visit www.internetvisitation.org and www.skype.com.

- **Rigidity** – If you have ever told the other parent, "You cannot see our daughter until six on Friday because that's what the court order says," you have not likely fully read and understood your order. The same holds true if you tell the other parent, "I don't care if he's at a birthday party. You better have him ready at six because that's what the court order says."

Prior to an order specifying parenting time, such as first, third, and fifth weekends, the language in most decrees states, "Failing mutual agreement," or "Absent mutual agreement." This basically means parents can modify the schedule as needed to meet their child's needs. Courts do not order rigid schedules that would be disadvantageous for children. Judge Diane Haddock says, "Standard visitation is for standard families, and I have not come across a single family that I would consider standard," and "Standard visitation is only a last resort, that's only failing agreements of the parties and failing more creative solutions."

Families and children need flexibility, just like they would have when all family members reside in one household. If you are child-focused (what's best for our child?) versus adult-focused (it's my period of "possession"), you will allow your child the maximum benefit of two homes and access to his or her entire family. Consider the standard court-ordered schedule as a fallback or back-up plan when no other mutual agreement is reached between you and your coparent. Your child will likely want to open up presents in both households on Christmas Day, and if both parents are child-focused, you can make that happen.

- **Letting Emotions Control You** – Remember from earlier in this book, who is responsible for every word that you utter or every behavior you engage in? You are. During alternative dispute-resolution sessions with the other parent, it is important to use your time and money effectively and productively. It will be natural to experience intense emotions during these sessions, and you may want to consult with a counselor to prepare for these meetings. Your emotions exist, but you can choose how to act in response to them. If you are struggling with your emotions, be sure to practice using "I" statements.

- **Outside Influence** – Recognize the "mouths" discussed earlier: they can derail the process by giving you counterproductive input during the dispute-resolution process. If you are going to listen to anyone, listen to the silent voice of your child. Wherever your child is right now, do you think your child is saying, "I want my family in conflict and I want a complete stranger tell me how I'm going to grow up"? Is your child saying, "I want to have a case worker ask me very personal questions about the adults in my life"? Is your child saying, "I want my family to spend my college education fund duking it out in court"? You know what your child is saying. Your child is saying, "If I'm going to grow up between two homes, I want a *family* to raise me, not litigants, and not judges."

Remember that in these alternative dispute-resolution meetings, you are planting the seeds for your child's future.

Chapter 5: The Use of Mental-Health Professionals

When you or your children are going through difficult periods, such as the transition to a two-home structure, seeking quality care and support is clearly a wise choice. Navigating the waters of difficult family transitions can be complex and burdensome, and counseling can often help families stay on course. Mental-health professionals can serve as therapists for you, your child, or your family. They can also assist with services such as mediation, cooperative parenting, and parenting coordination.

However, working with families raising children between two homes is an area of specialized training. I have seen many families damaged by the interference of unskilled practitioners who are not trained in this area of specialty and are not aware of the complexities of forensic (court connected) work. Unfortunately, I have dealt with cases where mental-health professionals "wore too many hats" with the family, made comments about a parent they never met, and/or made recommendations beyond the scope of their knowledge or ability.

It is important for you to know:

- As licensed professionals, mental-health professionals are required to provide services within the scope of minimum standards, but hopefully strive toward best practices. The Association of Family and Conciliation Courts (AFCC) has developed guidelines for mental-health professionals who work with coparenting families. These guidelines are available at www.afccnet.org/Resource-Center/Practice-Guidelines-and-Standards.

- In all circumstances, it is by definition the responsibility of the mental-health professional, not the client, to set and maintain appropriate professional boundaries.
- You put yourself at risk when you work with a professional who is not governed by a licensing board, as there is no entity overseeing that person's professional practice or conduct.
- In order to empower clients to make their own healthy decisions, professional codes of ethics generally discourage the self-disclosure of the mental-health professional's personal views. Be cautious of professionals who reveal in-depth information about their divorce, their history, or their personal circumstances. Generally, this may be assessed by visiting their website or in their advertisement.
- You have the right to file a complaint with the appropriate licensing board if you or your family members have received services from a licensed mental-health professional that do not meet the standards of care for the profession.
- You have the right to ask for proof of training before or during services.
- All licensed mental-health professionals have ethical guidelines they are expected to follow and state regulations they are required to follow. For example:
  - Psychologists: www.apa.org/ethics/code/index.aspx
  - Social workers: www.socialworkers.org/pubs/code/default.asp
  - Marriage and family therapists: www.aamft.org/imis15/content/legal_ethics/code_of_ethics.aspx
  - Professional counselors: www.counseling.org/knowledge-enter/ethics

Be sure the mental-health professional working with you and/or your child:

- Has read and follows the AFCC guidelines listed above for the role he or she is assuming with your family. You deserve best practices, not just minimum standards.
- Has experience with court-connected cases.
- Has training in coparenting issues and concerns such as cooperative parenting, alienation, estrangement, and family systems.

To the best of your ability, make sure the mental-health professional does *not*:

- Make definitive statements or recommendations about someone he or she has not met, such as your coparent. For example, there is a difference between saying, "Your coparent is obviously narcissistic, so what you need to do is..." versus "If what you're saying is accurate, that sounds to me like a narcissistic trait, and one way to respond to that might be...." The focus should be on helping you cope with issues, rather than labeling others with secondhand information.
- Wear too many hats, such as serving as your marriage therapist and then becoming your child's therapist.
- Make parenting-time schedule or custody recommendations, unless that person has or had an investigative forensic role (such as a custody evaluator).
- Attempt to have a therapeutic or treatment role if he or she had an investigative forensic role previously with you and/or your family. In other words, your evaluator should not later serve as your therapist or vice versa.

This concludes Part 1 of *Between Two Homes*. I hope I have helped you develop and label your emotionally healthy behaviors. I also hope I have challenged you to look at some things differently, provided new options you may not have considered, and given you new tools to use in your coparenting relationship. Part 2 focuses on the needs of children growing up between two homes.

PART 2 – CHILDREN'S ISSUES

Chapter 6: What to Expect

Statistically,* children growing up between two homes are at higher risk post separation for:

- Externalizing symptoms, such as disobedience, aggression, delinquency, temper tantrums, and over-activity.
- Internalizing symptoms, such as stomach problems, other physical complaints, worrying, and shyness.
- Greater academic and achievement problems.
- Substance abuse, teen pregnancy, depression, juvenile delinquency, and suicide.

So what can you do?

Hopefully, Part 2 of this book will help you better understand the needs of children growing up between two homes so that you can reduce the chances of your child suffering from these problems.

A great number of children thrive between two homes. Studies by both Paul R. Amato and E. Mavis Hetherington found that although many children experience short-term negative effects after a parental separation, these reactions typically diminish or disappear by the end of the second year. Only a minority of children growing up between two homes continue to struggle in comparison to children growing up in one home. Most children growing up between two homes also do well in the longer term. Some children, especially those where the original home was abusive, fared better post separation.

Part 2 of this book will help you recognize the risk factors for children growing up between two homes. These include:*

- Stress of the separation or family changes.

- Diminished parenting by either or both parents.
- Loss of relationships (with parents, extended family, or peers).
- High conflict between coparents, ongoing coparental litigation.
- Parents' new relationships.
- Incapacitated parenting due to substance abuse or mental illness.
- Distance between homes.
- Reduced or unstable economic resources.

It's also helpful to know which factors increase children's well-being when they are growing up between two homes. These include:*

- Good relationships with an adult or adults in one or both homes.
- Parental nurturance.
- Good sibling support.
- Protecting the children from coparental conflict.
- Frequent access to both parents when both parents are emotionally healthy.
- Access to both sides of the family.
- Competent parenting of both parents.
- Protecting the children from behaviors that place the children in the middle.

Common reactions for children experiencing significant family changes, such as divorce, include:*

- Anxiety and fear.
- Worry and confusion.
- Anger and sadness.
- Longing for one or both parents.
- Loneliness.
- Conflicted loyalties between homes.
- Guilt.

*(Amato and Cheadle, 2005; Hetherington and Stanley-Hagan, 1999; Johnston, 1994; Kelly and Emery, 2003; Laumann-Billings and Emery, 2000; Marquardt, 2005;

Pruett, Williams, Insabella, and Little, 2003; Wallerstein, Lewis, and Blakeslee, 2000)

Recognizing these reactions may help you to understand your child's behaviors and improve your communication with your child. Recognizing how further stress on your child exacerbates these reactions may also help you modify your counterproductive coparenting behaviors.

Children are affected by grief also, but how they process and respond to grief is very different than how adults do so. Most children show strong reactions to their parents' separation, especially over a period of one or two years following the separation. You might expect these reactions during these phases:

- **Shock and Denial** – They may have a shocked, flat affect (no display of emotions), may lie about the situation, or may ignore the situation.
- **Anger** – They may have more tantrums, be more dependent or clingy, and they may fight more with their siblings.
- **Bargaining** – They may act more responsible, play peacekeeper, try to help out more, promise to be better, earn better grades, and try to counsel the adults to stop the separation or divorce.
- **Depression** – They may start crying for no reason, pout more, lose interest in things they usually enjoy, or appear withdrawn. Their grades may decline and they may neglect chores. They may have physical complaints or lose their appetite. They may seek to be babied or pampered more and show regressive behaviors (such as acting younger than they are).
- **Acceptance** – Hesitantly at first, children may begin to talk more openly and freely about their disappointment. However, at this stage, they are more open to the changes and are better adjusted, possibly seeing new potential benefits of the situation. Their energy comes back, and they may return to doing fun activities or hobbies they enjoyed before.

Chapter 7: Talking to Your Child

Below are phrases parents sometimes use when explaining separation to a child, and why these phrases might cause problems for your child.

- "I don't love him/her anymore, so it's best we do this."
  (Your child may believe that you'll stop loving him or her one day too.)

- "Mommy and Daddy still love you, and it will be just like it's always been, except we'll live in different homes."
  (The problem is, it won't be just like it's always been, and your child may be confused regarding what's going to happen.)

- "Your mom wants this divorce, I don't. But there is nothing I can do about it."
  (Your child does not need to be involved in the finger pointing. Your child is not old enough to understand that separation and divorce are a consequences of an unhealthy relationship, not a cause.)

- "Remember how we disagreed about how we should take care of you? Well, now we are going to let the judge decide who was right."
  (Most people agree this is the wrong phrase to use because it gives the power of parenting to a stranger, but this phrase is an accurate description for some parents. However, it would not be helpful for your child to hear this.)

- "Everything will be all right, you'll see."
  (But it won't be. Your child will grieve and have some difficulty, and likely the parents will also. It's okay for your child to experience the grief and move through it.)

- "You can still see Dad whenever you want."
  (Parents have to work, children have to go to school, and other situations will arise where your child cannot see the other parent whenever he or she wants. In fact, children typically ask for their other parent when they are being disciplined.)

- "I will have my time with you, and Mom will have her time with you."
  (This sounds like your child is property. It would, however, be appropriate to say, "You will have time in both of your homes," or "You will spend private time with your mom and with your dad.")

- "Remember when you use to cry at night because we fought? Well that won't happen anymore."
  (This phrase will likely make your child feel responsible for the situation, and think "If I just had not cried, we would not be in this situation.")

So what is helpful to say in this situation?

- "Sometimes things just don't work out the way we plan them to. Things will be different, but we'll still love you."
  (This phrase, or any portion of this phrase, is recommended. Notice there is no blame placed on either parent. Also notice the use of "we" rather than "I," so your child is reassured you are both still his or her parents.)

By carefully choosing the words you use, you can help your child transition through these family changes. It is important to talk to your child about his or her experiences and to prepare your child for changes. Communication with your child allows you to understand your child's thoughts and feelings while allowing your child to feel heard and supported. Some of the things important to a child include:

- Understanding the appropriate details of the upcoming changes. What does it mean to now have two homes? Or in some cases, what does it mean to now have one home, but parents who come and go?
- Receiving an age-appropriate explanation for the situation that your child can understand.
- Being invited to ask questions.
- Receiving clarification that the situation is an adult decision made by parents and it is permanent. Your child has nothing to do with the reason for the situation and there is nothing your child can do to change it.
- Being invited to share what is important to your child and what your child wants or needs.
- Being invited to ask what your child thinks will make it easier for your child to have two homes.
- Reassuring your child of each parent's permanent roles (mother, father) and continuing relationship with him or her.
- Being listened to before, during, and after the changes.

It is also important for coparents to think carefully about how and what you both will tell your child about these changes. If possible and if it's safe, you can plan in advance what you will say to your child and then meet jointly with your child. Talk about how each of you will remain calm and avoid blame during the meeting. By meeting together with your child, you both can hear the same concerns and comments from your child and you both can answer your child's questions. This plan presents a united front for your child.

When talking to your child, **do not**:

- Assume your child is feeling or thinking the same

way you do about the situation.

- Involve your child in the dispute, no matter his or her age.
- Ask your child to choose sides.
- Blame either parent.
- Ask your child to make adult choices, such as who to live with, where he or she wants to live, or who he or she wants to spend more time with.
- Give your child false hope that the parents will reunite or some other unrealistic expectation.
- Give your child information about the adult intimate relationship, the adult conflict, or the legal dispute.
- Let your emotions get away from you.
- Say you are doing it for your child.
- Engage in conflict with your coparent.

A good communication tool when talking to your child, or your coparent for that matter, is the use of reflective listening. Reflective listening is asking a question or making a statement and adding a question after it for the purpose of clarification. Instead of trying to answer a question and "fix the problem," reflective listening allows you to clarify your understanding of the child's statement and assess the feeling underlying his or her statement. With reflective listening, you summarize what your child said, using your own words. For example:

Child: "I don't want you to separate. I don't want to be without either of you."

Parents: "I hear you saying you feel confused about how often you will see the two of us. Is that right?"

Child: "No. I don't know how much time I'll see you. It hurts thinking about not being with either of you."

Parents: "So I hear you are sad that you may miss time with either of us, and you are confused about how often you will see the two of us."

Child: "Yes!"

When talking to your child, **do**:

- Make sure you are having age-appropriate discussions, not ones that are over your child's head in relation to his or her maturity.
- Talk to your child using words that are age appropriate.
- Make sure your child knows it is not his or her fault and he or she had nothing to do with the situation, and he or she cannot change it.
- Let your child know both coparents and other family members love him or her.
- Let your child know the love that adults have for each other is very different than the love a parent feels for his or her child, which is never ending.
- Encourage your child to read age-appropriate books about the situation or read such books to him or her.
- Let your child know his or her basic needs will be met, that someone will still fix breakfast in the morning, help him or her do homework, and so on.
- Let your child know what will remain the same.
- Use reflective listening.

Chapter 8: Family Members

Siblings

Your children will likely benefit by having siblings who are sharing their experience of transition to two homes, and this experience may strengthen their bonds. As addressed earlier, the emotional stress that coparents feel following major family changes may temporarily reduce the amount of attention the parents are able to offer their children.

As a result, some children turn to one another for nurturance and support, or in some cases sibling rivalry may increase. Older children may want to take on the role of caretaker for the younger children to be the "man" or "woman" of the house. In some cases, the opposite occurs, and older children have less tolerance for the behaviors of their younger siblings. Younger children may compete for parental attention while older children may attempt to align the other children against a parent they "blame" for the separation. Confusion is not easy for a child to experience, and your child may express frustration to those your child feels closest to, such as a sibling.

Help siblings by:

- Maintaining continuity and tradition when possible.
- Maintaining consequences for unhealthy actions toward each other.
- Having family meetings and encouraging them to ask questions and share thoughts.
- Occasionally meeting with each child individually, and taking opportunities for special moments with him or her.
- Telling the children each one is important to you and your coparent.

- Telling all the children that the situation is not their fault, or any specific child's fault.
- Telling all the children that the situation is not their fault, or either parent's fault.
- Terminating behaviors of the older child attempting to be the "man" or the "woman" of the house, or to take on your duties and responsibilities.
- Reassuring your children that it is your job to take care of them, not their job to take care of you.
- Telling them they do not need to take sides, and that all the children are allowed to love both parents and the other adults in both homes.
- Not favoring one child over the other.
- Not splitting the children between homes (see "Mistake 12: Splitting Siblings" in Chapter 13).

Other Relatives

When children are growing up between two homes, their world can often become divided between maternal and paternal family members, or coparent A's family and coparent B's family. The children are allowed to interact with only coparent A's family during coparent A's parenting time, and with only coparent B's family during coparent B's parenting time. From your child's perspective, he or she has one big family involving all the family members. Stepfamily members may be an expansion to your child's family. You do a disservice to your child by not letting your child fully experience access to all their emotionally healthy family members. Some of the fondest memories most adults have are their childhood memories of times they spent with relatives.

Historically, our society understood the phrase, "It takes a village to raise a child." Your child can benefit from all the love, affection, and support offered by family members, and these extended family relationships should be facilitated, no matter whose parenting time it is. Not only do the children benefit from this; you may find your coparent's family members can be a great help to you when you need child care, support, or just extra hands at your child's birthday party.

Independent of your parenting time, help your child by:

- Allowing and encouraging your child to spend time and to communicate with all emotionally healthy family members.
- Inviting all family members to functions for your child, such as birthdays, extracurricular activities, and special events.
- Allowing your child to attend the functions of all their relatives, such as weddings, funerals, family reunions, and so on.
- If possible, asking your coparent's relatives to help out with party planning and child care.
- Thinking one big family, rather than maternal versus paternal.

To foster a "one big family" mentality, encourage your family members to stay out of the coparenting business between you and your coparent. You can remind them that their role as a relative to your child is more important than their role in supporting you, a grown adult. Encourage them to treat your coparent and your coparent's family with dignity, respect, and cooperation. Your family members do not have to like your coparent, but they can have the best relationship possible with your coparent for the sake of your child. If necessary, consider giving your relatives a copy of the coparenting supporters versus coparenting detractors page from Chapter 3.

Chapter 9: Age of Your Child

Children and their needs change from year to year. There are basic developmental considerations and norms for children at various ages that remain consistent from age to age and from one culture to the next.

I consider children growing up between two homes to be special needs children; the coparents have to work much harder between two homes to meet their child's developmental needs. The following section details the needs of children growing up between two homes, and what you want to consider regarding your child's needs during the different stages of your child's development.

0-18 Months

Especially during the first eighteen months, children need continuity in meals, rituals, environments, and bedtime. Parents create a schedule for the children that in turn creates a schedule for the parents. It benefits your child for both homes to have the same bedtime, naptime, and rituals. In the first years of life, your child experiences major development growth. He or she is learning to trust and form relationships with the people who take care of him or her. It is normal for children to bond to more than one person, such as to both parents in one home.

But physical care of your child is only one consideration. Emotional sensitivity and responding to your child's social needs, such as returning a smile or providing comfort when he or she is crying, are very important. Immediately after significant changes in the family take place, your infant may show his or her feelings through changes in behavior. Irritability, fussiness, gastrointestinal issues, and additional crying are possible reactions. He or she may experience difficulty in going from one parent to the other.

Pointers for ages birth to eighteen months:

- Routine is very important. Your child's daily schedule, including meals and sleep, should not vary drastically between homes.
- You and your coparent should agree whether your child will sleep in his or her own bed and bedroom, or in a bed or room with someone else, so that your child has the same experience in both homes.
- You should agree on the ritual prior to putting your child to bed. For example, there is a big difference between rocking him or her to sleep versus putting him or her in their crib and singing a lullaby for a few seconds before leaving.
- Care items, such as blankets or stuffed animals, should be exchanged or duplicated.
- If you argue, your child can detect that there is some tension but cannot understand the reasoning behind the conflict, so it is important to monitor your tone and body language.
- In regard to the schedule between the two homes, your child will need more frequent contact with both parents to maintain secure bonds, and less duration between contact with either parent. Your child will benefit from frequently hearing both parents' voices, feeling their touch, and smelling their parents' colognes and perfumes.

Focus on sleep situations:

Until about age ten, continuity in sleep situations between the two homes is preferred. Some cultures believe children should sleep with their parents until they wean themselves from this, while others believe children should never sleep with their parents, as it promotes dependency.

Bottom line for young children: it benefits your child if both households are on the same page. At young ages, children believe in the monster in the closet, under the bed, and outside their window, and that stuffed animals come to life.

Children sleeping alone develop one set of skills to comfort themselves to sleep at night, while children sleeping with someone else in their room become dependent on the security of having someone else there. Children being raised between two homes with different sleeping arrangements may experience greater insecurity at night. They may experience more fear, feelings of abandonment, or confusion, leading to a preference for being in one home or the other (typically the one where they share a room with someone) or difficulty transitioning between homes.

18 Months-3 Years

For children between eighteen months and three years old, routine in rules and expectations between the two homes is important. This is a difficult stage for parents and children, and often these years are described as "the terrible two's" and "tantrumy three's." Children have all these new abilities and do not know what to do with them. Imagine being a two year old who is encouraged to jump on furniture at one home, and punished for doing so at the other home. So, can your child jump on the furniture or not? If one parent says "yes" and the other "no," the parents could meet in the middle and buy an exercise trampoline for each home and then tell their child, "This is the one place you can jump inside the house."

Pointers for ages eighteen months to three:

- Your child is learning new vocabulary and new routines and is very dependent on parental guidance, so it's important that both homes provide the continuity and expectations of who this little child is learning to be.

- Expect an increase in sibling rivalry and demand on your time after a separation.
- Children are now generally more independent and may want to "do it myself."
- Keep normal schedules and routines in each home. Try not to change your patterns any more than necessary.
- Keep your child's favorite toys, blankets, or stuffed animals close at hand. Either let him or her carry these between homes or duplicate these items in both homes.
- Your child's sleeping arrangement remains important and should remain consistent between homes.
- Be patient with your child's fits. Allow your toddler to be upset.
- Do not change the rules just because of the transition to having two homes. Discipline as the two of you always have in the past, or if you never lived together, develop continuity in discipline.

3-6 Years

In elementary school, your children will begin to understand that changes in the living arrangement can be permanent. If your child is in this age group, he or she may take the blame for your situation. Your child may think, "Mom and Dad are fighting because I was bad." Although children in this stage have a better understanding than younger children of how their lives will be different because of the changes in living circumstances, your child may worry about the changes in his or her daily life and may experience more stress, which he or she may display by presenting difficulty with transitions between the homes or the start of having nightmares.

Your child may be sad because of a coparent's absence. Sometimes your child may be angry with the coparent he or she does not see as often. At other times, your child may be angry with the parent he or she may spend more time with. If your child is in preschool, he or she may be aggressive and angry toward one or both of you. You may also discover that your child has been making up stories about how you and your coparent are going to get back together or how you will all live in one home. Your child may also exaggerate his or her complaints about the other parent to get your attention.

Between three and six years old is the time when children experience social growth. Unfortunately, sometimes a parent does not want to promote this independence and social growth. This type of parent needs to be needed by the child. Such a parent can create difficulty for the child during exchanges by prolonging the exchange process.

There are ways parents can make transitions easier for children, as I cover in Chapter 10. Remember to make it about your child (making it easy for your child to go) and not about you (and how hard it is to let your child go).

Pointers for children ages three to six:

- Make transitions easier for children by making the exchange as smooth and brief as possible.
- Children may be afraid of monsters at this age, so their sleeping situation continues to remain important.
- Your child is moving out into the world more with child care and school, so try not to overwhelm him or her with multiple daycares, schools, new relationships, and child care providers.
- Use flexibility in the schedule between homes if your child appears to really want to spend time with his or her other parent or family members.
- Watch what you say and do. Your child now understands words, and not only will he or she experience stress when you disparage your coparent, but your child is likely to repeat your comments to your coparent.

- Read books to your child about two-home matters, and encourage your child to share feelings and thoughts about the books.

6-12 Years

Children six to twelve years old are fun to be around. Our inner child likes to play with them, and they can be independently responsible as well. However, this is the time when I see children's needs most neglected by the legal term, "My period of possession." Parents need to see this time as "parenting time" or "periods of responsibility." To a child, "period of possession" means "This parent is going to take care of me" not "This parent owns me during this time."

Children need to have peer relationships and extracurricular activities. So if it is your weekend and your child is enrolled in soccer, where are you and where is the child? Your answer should be, "At the soccer game." If your child wants to spend the night with a best friend living near the other parent, your child should be able to do this often. You child should be able to attend peer birthday parties independent of whose parenting time it is.

Pointers for children ages six to twelve:

- Be sure to explain to your child that he or she is not responsible for the current situation. You will likely need to say this many times.
- Explain who will take care of your child and what changes will (or can) happen.
- Talk with your child about his or her feelings and thoughts; be sensitive to your child's fears.
- Help your child feel good about both you and your coparent as much as possible. Make it a point to say positive things about your coparent regularly.
- A large part of your child's focus is now on peer relationships and extracurricular activities. This is the time parents will need to focus more on their

"period of responsibility" instead of their "period of possession."

- While both parents need to support the educational and extracurricular activities of their child, both parents also need to mutually agree on extracurricular activities prior to enrolling their child, especially if the activity may occur during the other parent's parenting time.

- In addition to one-on-one time with your child, part of being a responsible parent is transporting your child to and from activities, sitting on the sidelines during his or her events, and making sure your child spends time with friends. Your child may have first, third, and fifth weekend parents, or second and fourth weekend parents, but that doesn't mean they have first, third, and fifth weekend friends and activities, and different second and fourth weekend friends and activities.

Teenagers

Teenagers are most concerned about who they are from their perspective, and they are not as concerned about their time with parents. They are taking the early steps of independence.

The schedule between homes needs to be flexible with input from your child, but not so as to cut off your child's frequent access to *both* parents. Parents become less active in doing things for their child and more active in the facilitation of their teen's development. In other words, the parents' roles during the teenage years often seem to shift to chefs, taxi drivers, and bankers and away from one-on-one time with their teenager.

Blaming is often an automatic reaction for a teen. It's easy to blame a parent for something (or to blame someone else, such as the people in the teen's other home) when he or she is upset. Blaming can also serve as a quick fix that leaves your teen feeling more in control, which is especially tempting if your teen feels that this behavior will give him or her a say in the decisions you are making. In other words, teens will often try to play homes against each other. If you can't or don't know how to make things better for your teen, don't make matters worse by letting him or her drive the bus.

Pointers for children ages twelve to eighteen:

- Friends and extracurricular activities become even more important, so both parents need to be flexible when scheduling parenting time. Both parents need to be willing to take responsibility as taxi drivers, bankers, and chefs.
- Both parents need to understand that there will be times when other significant family events, such as weddings or funerals, will prevent their children from attending activities.
- Teenagers' schedules do not fit into standard parenting schedules very well. This may mean your child spends a little more time with one parent because of extracurricular involvement, or it may mean your child spends more time with peers. Your child may even have a job.
- Don't be mistaken; your teenager's independence does not mean your pre-teen or teen rules the roost. Unless there is abuse, your child should never be allowed to dictate whether to see one parent or the other, any more than you would allow your child to choose whether to come home if he or she lived in one home. If you tell your child that he or she has a choice to be with the other parent, the message your child may get is that he or she has the choice to be with either parent... or neither parent. If this happens, you may end up with a child who runs away, a child who looks to gangs, or a child who experiences early pregnancy in his or her search for the authority lacking at home.
- Teens will often play parents against each other when they can if it benefits them.

Because they are older and look like young adults, it is easy for some parents to pull teenagers into adult issues or adult roles.

- Do not rely on your teen for emotional support. Spare your teen that additional emotional burden and responsibility.
- Do not manipulate, apply pressure, or lie to make your teen take sides or to support you over your coparent.
- Do not expose your teen to your arguments, abusive behavior, or conflicts with your coparent.
- Do not argue or become angry with your teen about how he or she feels. All feelings, justified or not, need to be acknowledged and processed.

Chapter 10: The Schedule Between Homes

"Just remember that your child is a unique individual, that they will develop at the rate that they need to develop at, and you need to make changes that accommodate them." —Judge Judith Wells

A large source of conflict for many coparents is the schedule between the two homes. If both parents do not agree on the schedule, both parents often think, "The schedule I'm proposing is the best for the children and the other parent is wrong." Bear in mind that it is impossible to come up with the perfect plan for all children at all ages. I encourage you to take a minute and put yourself in your children's shoes. Would you at your age right now want to be:

- In town A Monday through Wednesday, then town B on Thursday, then back to A on some weekends, then back to town B on other weekends. Then on the following week Monday through Wednesday in town A, then Thursday through Monday morning in town B?
- In town A Monday through Tuesday, then town B on Wednesday through Thursday, then rotating weekends between towns?
- One week in town A and one week in town B?

Would you want to live with any of these plans? Think about how these plans would affect your work, your study habits, your relationships with friends, and your dating life. Now, imagine I came up to you and said I created one of these plans in your best interest. Would you believe me? The reality is, these schedules are not created for the best interests of children; these schedules are created because of adult circumstances that create two homes.

While I refer to "two homes" throughout this book, it's important to note that sometimes it's the parents who have two homes rather than their child. Not all parents have their children moving between two homes.

In some cases, parents do what is commonly called *nesting,* in which case the child stays in one household the entire time, and the parents do the moving in and out. Generally, one parent is in the house with the children for one week while the other parent resides somewhere else. The next week, the opposite occurs. Their child keeps his or her own room, toys, pets, neighborhood, and sense of place. The child gets off the same school bus every day and has the same neighborhood friends. Many parents find that it's cheaper to have two small apartments and one large house rather than try to maintain two large houses, and some save more by staying with relatives or friends on their off nights.

In other cases, parents live around the block (or a short walk or bicycle ride away) and the parents stay in one home the entire time, but their child is so close to each home that he or she ebbs and flows between the homes. Basically, if the child runs out of peanut butter in one home, he or she can dash over to the other home. In such a situation, there is rarely a need for a rigid schedule such as first, third, and fifth weekends, because the child is actively at both homes on a regular basis.

One hundred and fifty years ago, parents rarely divorced, and the maternal and paternal grandparents (or other relatives) lived in close proximity to the parents. Children often spent time with their grandparents on a daily or weekly basis, and everyone understood the concept addressed earlier in this book: "It takes a village to raise a child." Though children often spent a great deal of time in one home, they also spent a great deal of time in another home. There was no rigid schedule.

However, due to the gradual increase in social mobility, most families have become more of a nuclear family, with relatives living far off. With today's increased divorce rates, the nuclear family is often cut in half, and some parents are now trying to divide their children's time into maternal and paternal time.

Of course, the greater the distance between two homes, the more difficult it will be for your child to spend time in both homes as freely as possible.

When designing a schedule between two homes for your child, it's important to consider the following:

- Enhancing the quality of the relationship between the parent and child is important in determining the amount of time between homes.
- Avoid rigid schedules.
- Frequent contact with both parents is linked to better adjustment when both parents are emotionally healthy.
- There is no one schedule that is right for all children at all times at all ages, and a good plan changes to address the child's development.

Deterrents to children wanting to spend time with a parent include:

- Witnessing or experiencing violence.
- Emotional abuse.
- That parent being self-absorbed.
- A parent's preoccupation with dating.
- Rigid or punitive parenting.
- Alienation by the other parent.

Additional things to consider include:

- The child's age, maturity, temperament, and strength of attachment to each parent.
- Any special needs of the child and parents.
- The child's relationship with siblings and friends.
- The distance between the two households.
- The flexibility of both parents' work schedules.
- Childcare arrangements.
- Transportation needs.

- The ability of the parents to communicate and cooperate.
- The child's and parents' cultural and religious practices.
- A parent's willingness to provide adequate supervision and care even if the parent has not done so in the past.

Suggestions to consider in developing a schedule between homes that will change depending on your child's age include:

0-3	More frequent contact with both parents such as every other day, and less time between seeing either parent. Developmentally, a child bonded to both parents can spend the night between two homes.
3-5	Children are able to increase time away from either parent and spend ample time overnight in both homes.
5-8	Allow flexibility in the schedule when needed.
8-18	Incorporate peer and extracurricular activities during either parent's parenting time.

Exchanging your child between homes may become an increasingly difficult experience for your child. The following tips may make it easier on your child during exchanges. Suggestions from a child's point of view include:

- Have me ready to go at the time designated.
- If you are coming to get me, pick me up on time so I don't sit around waiting and worrying. If you are running late, let my other parent know in advance or

as soon as you can.
- Set up a routine that usually occurs before I leave
- Remind me at least twenty minutes before the exchange to pack items I may want to take.
- Don't make me carry a suitcase of things I couldn't care less about, such as toothpaste, toothbrushes, underwear, and so on. These things should already be in both of my homes for me.
- If I have difficulty with separation, consider having the parent whose time with me is ending deliver me to the other parent.
- If I am excited and run out the door to take off with my other parent, don't call me back to give you a hug or kiss.
- Don't tell me you will miss me; just tell me that you love me.
- Be polite during the exchange; do not argue or fight.
- Don't tell me to give something to my other parent or to deliver a message to my other parent.
- If it is safe, walk up to my door when you come to get me, don't just pull up and honk or call/text my other parent (or me).
- If I want to allow my other parent to see my room or something I am doing, allow me to let them in as long as it is safe.
- Do talk to my other parent about any homework I may have or medication I need. Do not leave this up to me, because I am a child and I have a hard time keeping up with these things... or I may not want to.
- Try not to exchange me at a fast food or gas station parking lot. Exchange me at my homes or when I get out of school or extracurricular activities.

Chapter 11: Maintaining Continuity Between Homes

Parenting between two homes does not end at your doorstep; it extends into your child's other home and into the coparenting relationship. Your child will benefit from continuity and consistency in parenting between homes. Focus on your house being "one of your child's homes" instead of "my home."

Let's see how easy it is to fall into "my home" thinking. Answer this question: At what age is a child delayed if he or she is not independently walking?

When I ask this question during my live coparenting class, parents answer anywhere between nine and seventeen months.

So, what is the difference between the ages mentioned?

For the mathematicians reading this book, your answer is, "eight months," but that is not the point of this question. The answer is *it's only a difference of opinion.*

But when it comes to custody cases, sometimes a parent will appear before the court and say, "I'm the better parent because I removed the walker at ten months." The other parent says, "I'm not going to force my son to develop too quickly, so I'm letting him use the walker." This is an example of "mom's house" versus "dad's house" thinking, instead of the two parents being united to create consistency for their child.

I encourage you not only to remove the phrases "mom's house," "dad's house," and "my house" from your vocabulary, but also to remove these ideas from your way of thinking. As mentioned earlier in this book, changing your thinking can change your behavior.

If you think of your house as "my house," it is easier to

reject your child's request to let your coparent come see something in your child's room. If you think about the house as "your child's other home," it may be easier for you to allow your child have your coparent come see what is in your child's room (as long as it is safe). Your child will benefit from your creating two homes united in the best interests of your child and from your creating continuity and consistency between those homes.

However, sometimes parents start dressing their child up in little "uniforms" very early on in the separation process. Basically, the child hears:

Parent A: What are you wearing, that green uniform? I thought I sent you over in the orange uniform. As long as you are in my house, I expect you to wear an orange uniform. I expect you to act this way, not that way, have these religious beliefs, not those religious beliefs, and keep up with these chores no matter what your chores are in your other home. I expect you to eat this diet, not that diet, have this routine, not that routine, think this way, not that way. As long as you are in *my* house, I expect you to act, perform, and think this way, and if you don't, I'm going to be very disappointed in you, and, in fact, I might even punish you.

Then the child goes to the other house and hears:

Parent B: What are you wearing, that orange uniform? I thought I sent you over in the green uniform. As long as you are in my house, I expect you to wear a green uniform. I expect you to act this way, not that way, have these religious beliefs, not those religious beliefs, and keep up with these chores no matter what your chores are in your other home. I expect you to eat this diet, not that diet, have this routine, not that routine, think this way, not that way. As long as you are in *my* house, I expect you to act, perform, and think this way, and if you don't, I'm going to be very disappointed in you, and, in fact, I might even punish you.

Unfortunately, some parents do not understand their child's need for continuity and instead think, "I don't care how the other parent does it in their house, this is my house, and I get to parent my way." These parents often spend time with coparenting detractors rather than coparenting supporters. These parents can create great difficulties for their child. When professionals interview these children, the question is not, "Where are you today— are you in your home with your mom or your dad?" But instead, "Who are you today?" because these children explain that they have to be a different person in each home.

Now answer this question: At what age do you think children should be potty trained?

When I ask this question during my live coparenting class, parents answer anywhere between two and five years old.

In the "mom's house" versus "dad's house" pattern, one house offers the daughter a choice of diapers or pull-ups. So she picks diapers. That parent pats the child on the head and says, "Whatever you want, sweetie." The child goes to her other house in diapers. That parent says, "Big girls don't wear diapers; big girls wear pull-ups." Now what do you think this child is feeling? When she returns to the home where she has a choice, what is she most likely going to pick? Most likely she will pick the pull-ups, because she was told her last decision was a bad one, and a big girl would not have made that choice.

Either style of potty-training is appropriate, but it needs to be consistent. In this case, these parents are not acting as "coparents," and they are not providing a consistent experience for their child. Unfortunately, these differences can continue as children get older, with vast differences between the parents and their perceptions of who their child is, what their child is to believe, and who their child is to grow into.

To create consistency between two homes, it's important that the coparents examine their parenting style. Research* has identified four parenting styles:

- **Indulgent parents** (also referred to as "permissive," "nondirective," or "laissez-faire") according to Baumrind (1991) "are more responsive than they are demanding. They are nontraditional and lenient, do not require mature behavior, allow considerable self-regulation, and avoid confrontation." The parents often respond to their children's wishes, even when these wishes are unreasonable or inappropriate. Punishments are seldom threatened, let alone carried through, and the children often appear to have the upper hand in the relationship. Indulgent parents may be further divided into two types: a) democratic parents, who, though lenient, are more conscientious, engaged, and committed to the child, and b) nondirective parents.

- **Authoritarian parents** are highly demanding and directive, but not responsive. Baumrind (1991) says of these parents: "They are obedience- and status-oriented, and expect their orders to be obeyed without explanation." They intervene frequently, issuing commands, criticisms, and occasional praise, but do this in an inconsistent way. They expect their children to obey their instructions without explanation, and may use emotional tactics to get their way, such as making their children feel guilty, ashamed, or unloved. Authoritarian parents can be divided into two types: a) nonauthoritarian-directive, who are directive, but not intrusive or autocratic in their use of power, and b) authoritarian-directive, who are highly intrusive.

- **Authoritative parents** are both demanding and responsive. Baumrind (1991) describes authoritative parents as ones who "Monitor and impart clear standards for their children's conduct. They are assertive, but not intrusive and restrictive. Their disciplinary methods are supportive, rather than punitive. They want their children to be assertive as well as socially responsible, and self-regulated as well as cooperative." Authoritative parents monitor their children and intervene when necessary, but let them get on with things when there is no need to interfere. They mean what they say, and do not shy away from conflict when enforcing the boundaries they have set. Authoritative parents are loving but not overindulgent, involved but not overly controlling, clear about limits but not excessively risk-averse, and permissive within those limits but not neglectful.

- **Uninvolved parents** are both unresponsive and undemanding. In extreme cases, this parenting style might encompass both rejecting-neglecting and neglectful parents, although most parents of this type fall within the normal range. These parents are unresponsive, undemanding, permissive, and set few clear boundaries, largely because they don't really care very much. Unlike authoritative parents, they are neither warm nor firm, and they do not monitor their children. Instead, they are laid-back and unresponsive to an extent that can sometimes seem reckless. In extreme cases, uninvolved parenting may stray into outright neglect.

So what is the best style to use in both homes? While each child is different, research* has shown that the **authoritative style** produces children who turn out well. They are responsible, obedient when they need be, independent at other times, and successful in school both academically and socially.

Uninvolved parenting is most strongly associated with problems in childhood development. Children who receive such parenting do poorly in many areas and often engage in delinquent behavior and/or substance abuse as adolescents.

Authoritarian parenting produces children who tend to be aggressive, have low self-esteem, do not relate well to peers, and are anxious.

Indulgent parenting produces children who are aggressive, impulsive, irresponsible, and disobedient in school.

*(Baumrind, 1991; Chao, 2001; Cohen and Rice, 1997; Park and Bauer, 2002; Steinberg, Mounts, Lamborn, and Dornbusch, 1991)

Again, coparenting does not end at your doorstep but instead continues into your child's other house. Good coparenting requires communication between homes. So, do you think the following is a good example of coparenting communication?

"I went to the store and bought a sippy cup. I introduced it to our daughter, and she's doing fine, so I'm sending one for you to use in your house."

If you think about it, this statement may sound like you're being helpful (you did buy another sippy cup, after all) but you're actually telling the other parent you made a decision for your child and you expect your coparent to follow your instructions. One pebble in a stream does not create a dam, but many pebbles do. Each time you make a statement that to your coparent appears to be an order, it is yet another pebble in the stream, and it can set up a dam in the coparenting relationship.

A good example of coparenting communication is, "I was thinking of buying sippy cups for our daughter to use in both of our homes. I think she's old enough to be introduced to it. What do you think?" Instead of setting up a dam, you are encouraging the other parent to make shared decisions with you about your child.

If one parent says to start using the sippy cup at five months, and the other parent says eight months, then the compromise could be six and half months. Of course, you don't always need to meet in the middle. If you explore interests versus positions, it's much easier to come to a solution. One parent could just do it the other parent's way, but at least both parents were offered a voice. The parents may decide not to use a sippy cup at all.

I'm going to use two towns (Minneapolis and St. Paul) as an analogy to discuss house rules, or "the laws of the land." When I'm describing these differences, I'm referring to the rules between your child's two homes, such as bedtime, consequences, and chores. I'm not referring to the "flavor" between your child's two homes. Flavor differences between two homes can be good for children. For example, one house may be more outdoor-physical and the other more indoor-artistic. This is good; both flavors enhance your child's identity. One household may be Spanish-speaking and the other English-speaking. Great! Your child will be bilingual.

It would be pretty easy for two parents to make two households fifty percent the same and fifty percent different, but who would it complicate life for? *Your child.*

If you make it so that seventy percent of the rules are the same and only thirty percent are different, who does that challenge? *You and your coparent.* But whose quality of life improves? *Your child's.*

So if both homes make it so that ninety percent of the rules are the same and only ten percent are different, who is really challenged? *You and your coparent.* But whose quality of life vastly improves? *Your child's,* the very person who you would be willing to do just about anything for.

Just as the laws between Minneapolis and Saint Paul are very similar, the rules between two homes can be similar also. Those rules include what is an acceptable behavior, what is an unacceptable behavior, and what is the consequence for that unacceptable behavior. Successful coparents can create a behavioral chart to use in both homes. There are online programs to help parents do this. Some parents use carry-over discipline so that if a child is grounded in one household the consequence is carried over to the other home.

Obviously, it is better for your child to be raised between two similar homes, but if you choose not to put that in place for your child, I encourage you to at least make the difference no more than the difference between states in the United States, for example, California and Florida, and preferably no more than the difference between two cities in the same state. Put yourself in your child's shoes. Forget the travel time and think just about the laws of the land. Would you rather go back and forth on a weekly basis between Minneapolis and St. Paul or Florida and California? *Who do you belong to? What is your culture? Can you have the bumper sticker "I'm proud to be a Floridian" when you go to California? How would you feel?* The laws are different, the politics are different, the lay of the land is different, and the culture and climate are different. *Who are you going to cheer for at football games?* It would be far more difficult for you as a child to live between Florida and California than it would be for you to live between Minneapolis and St. Paul.

Unfortunately, some children are forced into the following analogy: Mexico versus England. These children have been raised in one home with one set of rules until the parents decide to separate. It is now "mom's house" versus "dad's house."

Imagine what would it be like for you at your age right now to be forced to move to Mexico tomorrow? How long would it take to feel at home? (Two years to never.) How different are the languages, the laws, the culture, or the way you may perceive Mexican food to be? What is it really like in Mexico?

Now imagine that on Thursday nights and first, third, and fifth weekends, you are in England. Different language, different laws, government, climate, and so on. You now have a king or queen. Even something as basic as driving is different!

In Mexico and the United States, people drive on the same side of the road, but in England, people drive on the opposite side of the road. Adults drive without consciously thinking about it all the time; we go on automatic pilot. We find ourselves putting on the brakes when we see a police officer. We accidentally take the exit to our old employer, or we may drive our elementary school student to the high school because we are in a rush. So you can imagine how that tendency may increase the likelihood of a car accident or breaking the law if you were regularly driving between Mexico and England.

Officials in these countries have the right to tell you to do it their way; after all, you are an adult and you chose to be in that country. But should you have the same expectations of your child, who never asked to have two homes in the first place? Children are often caught up in similar differences because parents have started thinking "mom's house" and "dad's house" instead of "what are we going to do to create consistency in our child's two homes?"

So how can you work together to create consistency? Imagine you find out the other parent purchased a NERF ball and allows your child to throw it in the house in the other home. You now find yourself holding a NERF ball that has been thrown at you by your child, but you do not want your child throwing the ball inside the house. Instead of punishing your child for violating your household rule, what do you do? You could tell your child, "Good throw. I'm afraid I'm going to break something if we play ball inside. Let's take the ball outside and play." Later, call your coparent and see if an agreement can be reached on a rule regarding playing ball inside the house. Unfortunately, many parents do not take the time to consider creating continuity between homes.

It can become extremely confusing and frustrating for a child when that child's parents are more focused on each parent's comfort and need for control than on the child's need for continuity and consistency. When parents continue to think "mom's house" versus "dad's house," the differences between expectations in homes may continue to expand over time, with even more change in the rules. Just when a child thinks he or she understands the rules between homes, the rules start changing again. And what's one big reason why the rules would suddenly change?

Suppose Mexico starts dating and marries Japan, while England starts dating and marries Spain. Each country has different laws. So now the rules in both homes change again!

In this situation, the parents aren't focused on the needs of their child. Instead, the parents are trying to please themselves in this situation, thinking, "If I do it stepmom's way, I get a lot more of what I want out of this relationship and *we* are happier." Some parents make the excuse that they are trying to please the stepparents, but in reality, pleasing the stepparent pleases that parent.

The following table illustrates how this switch can occur.

When parents live together	#1 Your child's best interest #2 The parent's interest
Mom's house, dad's house thinking	#1 The parent's interest #2 Your child's best interest
Changing the rules when a parent remarries	#1 The parent's interest #2 The stepparent's interest #3 Your child's best interest

It certainly does not have to be this way. Work with the other household to create similar rules between homes to the best of your ability. Marry a person who supports this need for your child. Emotionally healthy stepparents will support your maintaining the rules your child was raised with rather than trying to enforce their will on your child.

I want you to raise your child between Minneapolis and St. Paul, (rather than between California and Florida or between Mexico and England). That means I encourage you to date only people who either already live in Minneapolis or St. Paul, or are willing to move there.

Imagine you go on a date with Mr. or Ms. Canada. Your date is so sexy, so funny, makes plenty of money, and you are incredibly attracted to him or her. You explain that you are working with your coparent to raise your child between Minneapolis and St. Paul, and your date's response is, "Minneapolis–St. Paul? I could never live there. I don't like their religious beliefs, I don't like their style of discipline, and I don't like the way they feed, clothe, or bathe their children."

As attracted to your date as you are, for the sake of your

child, what could you say? Try, "Goodbye. It was nice to meet you. The more you talk about Canada the better it sounds, and when my youngest child turns eighteen, I hope you're still single, but I've already made a commitment to my child and I need to respect that commitment before I create new commitments based on my desire to be in a new relationship."

Now, if Mr. or Ms. Canada says, "Well, I'm a pretty flexible person. Let's just see where this goes. Over time, we should be able to see if I can support your parenting style," that is a good sign. At least your date is being honest. And then test over a period of months whether what they've said is true, certainly before introducing your child to him or her.

Now what if Mr. or Ms. Canada says, "Great! I'll move to St. Paul tomorrow"? Be very cautious; this could be a dangerous sign. Some people will tell you anything on that first date, but several months later, you may see their jealousy or their need to control rise, and then they'll try to interfere in your coparenting relationship by becoming coparenting detractors, as described in Chapter 3. For example, if you are trying to talk on the phone to your coparent, a coparenting detractor may start whispering to you what to tell the other parent, or passing notes to you, or even eventually start making the calls or proofing and sending the e-mails for you to your coparent. This is a bad sign.

Chapter 12: Creating a Coparenting Plan

So how do you create and maintain consistency and continuity between homes?

You and your coparent can create a coparenting plan. Often what I see in my work with families is that families do not plan ahead. They wait until something is not working to address the problem. Or, they proceed on assumptions, which may result in more conflict and lead to more litigation.

A plan helps provide a roadmap for others. For example, a stepmother would likely not cut her stepdaughter's hair to her ears when it's been at her waist if the parents have an agreement that states, "The parents must mutually agree to significant changes in the child's physical or cosmetic appearance."

A good parenting plan:

- Is a written plan.
- Provides future solutions to help parents avoid pitfalls.
- Promotes trust.
- Promotes continuity and stability.
- Helps stepparents and other family members by providing a road map.

A coparenting plan is a contract agreed to by you and your coparent that establishes guidelines both homes will follow.

Bear in mind that people change. Rules change, living situations change, and people move on to new relationships. A coparenting plan addresses many of these pitfalls and helps keep you out of court and out of conflict with the other parent. Because dividing time between adults requires a great deal of trust between the coparents, a coparenting plan in a large way promotes this security because you have agreed on certain guidelines. The age of the child, of course, has a great bearing on how detailed you need to be in terms of your plan. Young children *need* consistency between homes. Older children are more adaptable, but may require more rules.

Coparenting plans help future relationships because the plan allows the significant others in your present or future to read what you agreed on and decide whether they can honor that agreement. If not, they are not likely the right choice to be a stepparent. Additionally, you will be less prone to follow a different path when you have a plan of action.

It would be very difficult for someone else to create the best parenting plan for each of you and your child. Coparenting plans are created to document the ongoing coparenting and family rules that do not and should not end just because an intimate relationship has ended or because there is conflict between the coparents. Even the "experts" don't always agree on very important issues that are fundamental to coparenting. For example, what type of discipline is best, should the child sleep with you or not, and so on.

When creating a parenting plan, a good question to ask yourself is, "How would we have handled this if we both lived together?" Generally, if the answer now differs because there are two homes, ask yourself, "Why is it better for our child to do this differently?" and "Is it possible to handle the situation the same way we would have if we lived together?" For example, examine such questions as:

- Who do I ask to watch our child if I can't be with the child during my parenting time? Generally, if you still lived together, you'd ask your coparent first before you asked family, friends, a nanny, or a babysitter.

- Would I let our child spend time with friends if I were seeing him or her every day? Generally, yes, you would. In fact, you'd probably be saying, "Go out and play."
- Where would our child sleep if we still lived together? The way you did it before should be continued unless both parents mutually agree otherwise.

You know your child better than anyone else, and both parents know what direction they want to raise the child in. A coparenting plan should cover at least some of the following areas and provide answers to the following questions:

- **Bed Time and Routines** – Bath before bed? Reading before bed? Where does your child sleep, alone or with someone? Does your child use a blanket or pacifier? Does your child sleep in a crib or bed? What do you do in the middle of the night when your child cries; do you put your child in your bed, or do you comfort your child to sleep in his or her own bed? Does your child listen to music while going to sleep? Does your child have a nightlight?
- **Discipline** – Rewards and punishment: How do you give praise: vocally, or through gifts, an allowance, charts, and so on? What are the consequences for behaviors you do not want your child to engage in? Do you use corporal punishment? Do you give your child a time-out, send your child to his or her room, put your child in the corner, ground him or her (and if so, for how long and for what consequences), do you remove some of your child's privileges, and so on? Will you use carry-over discipline between the two homes? (For example, if the child has been grounded in one home and the grounding period isn't over before the exchange, does the grounding carry over to the other home?) Will you use a behavioral chart in both homes?
- **Relationships** – If you are not divorced, should you

wait until after the divorce is finalized prior to introducing your child to a new significant other, and if so, how long after? What is the minimal time you date someone prior to introducing or reintroducing your child to that person? What do you want to make sure potential significant others know about your agreement before they decide to become involved? Will you define what terms your child may use when referring to stepparents (first name, Mom/Dad, or Stepmom/Stepdad), or will you allow your child to make that decision?

- **Daily Routines** – For younger children, what are the daily routines? What baby care products do you use? What diapers? What formulas? When do you switch foods? When and how do you potty train? Will you use a pacifier or walker? What is your child's bedtime? Will your child sleep with adults or in his or her own room?
- **Illness** – If your child is sick, do you still exchange? Should you keep a medicine checklist, so you are giving medicines about the same time and noting reactions to the medications? Should each of you be able to attend doctor's appointments, and should each of you be notified in advance (barring an emergency) of upcoming appointments?
- **Special Needs** – Does your child have special needs? Do both coparents need to attend child-related appointments together? Will your child's special needs affect the schedule between homes? Do you need to duplicate medical items, such as nebulizers? Will one parent be the primary caretaker, or will you both be equal caretakers?
- **Cell phone and Internet** – At what age, if ever, do you both agree you will allow your child to have a cell phone or access the Internet? What are the rules in both homes for cell phone and Internet usage? Can either of you post pictures of or information about your child on the Internet, and if so at what age and what kind of information?
- **Extracurricular Activities** – Do you both need to

agree per enrollment period before enrolling your child, especially in events that might occur during the other parent's parenting time? Do you both need to agree prior to removing your child from an activity? Should you tell your child you support an activity before you talk to the other parent? If an event, such as a wedding, occurs during the other parent's parenting time, should your child be excused from his or her extracurricular activity?

- **Religion** – Will your child be raised in one faith, two faiths, or with no religious training? Will those values change, depending on who each parent is in a relationship with? Are there specific religious days that need to be incorporated into your plan? Are there specific values you want to incorporate into your plan? Do you need to mutually agree on religious activities and practices?

- **Supervision** – What are your limits on adult supervision of your child? Can your child ride bicycles in the street alone? Can your child run down the block to a neighbor's? Does your child need to check in with you upon arrival? Who are considered appropriate supervisors for the child? (All relatives, some relatives?) Do nannies or babysitters have to be approved by both parents before being hired? At what age can your child be left home alone and for how long?

- **Terminology** – What words will you use ("visiting," "living with," "when you are at your other home")? Will you refer to the other parent as "her mother/father" or as "my ex?"? What terms are appropriate for each parent and for other relatives?

- **Peer Relationships** – Can your child still have sleepovers and independent relationships with friends near the home of their mother/father during the other parent's parenting time?

- **Other Family Members** – Will your child be able to see all family members independent of which parent he or she is with, or will your child spend time only with maternal family during maternal time and vice versa? Will all family members be invited to your child's birthday parties? Are there family members your child should not see or who your child should always be supervised with?

- **Child Care** – Will you use one child-care provider, daycare, and nanny, or two? What age does a child-care provider need to be? Should you offer the other parent the opportunity to care for your child before you offer it to anyone else? Does the "anyone else" include grandparents, stepparents, and live-ins or not? Do you offer the opportunity for a span of two hours or more, or only if you will be gone overnight?

- **Trips** – If your child will be out of the area during your parenting time, do you need to provide your coparent with the basic travel itinerary? If so, what needs to be included in the notice? How far in advance do you need to provide the information? At what age can your child travel alone?

- **Professional Services** – Who will make decisions regarding the professionals who provide services for your child? Will those decisions be made jointly or by just one parent? Will one parent make the education decisions and the other the medical? Should both parents be listed as contacts on professional forms completed for your child?

- **Online tools** – Will you both use online tools to help you in shared parenting? Will you use e-mail to communicate agreements? Will you use any coparenting programs, such as www.ourfamilywizard.com?

- **Distance** – Will you have a geographical restriction regarding where your child will reside? Will there be a maximum distance between the two homes?

- **Schedule** – What schedule will your child have between the two homes? Will the school year schedule be different than the summer schedule? Will the schedule change as your child matures? What voice, if any, will your child have in that schedule? Does the schedule change depending on the distance between homes?

- **Holiday Schedules** – How do you celebrate? Will one parent have Christmas Eve and the other Christmas Day? Do you rotate Christmas Day and Eve with one parent one year and the other the next? Which holidays do you observe? Do you have religious issues related to holidays? What will be the schedule on your child's birthdays or on either parent's birthday? What will you do when there are federal holidays or when school is not in session due to a teacher in-service day?

- **School Work and Study Habits** – Will you use the same routine in both homes for dealing with homework or studies? How do you handle a project that may take longer than a day for your child to complete? If necessary, does that project transfer between homes?

- **Car** – Do you need to create a mutually agreed upon driving contract for your teen? Will the car be the teen's car, or will it be a car you are letting them borrow? Will the teen's behavior affect his or her use of the vehicle? Who will teach your teen to drive?

- **Child's Property** – What do you do with your child's clothes? Do each of you keep equal stock, or does one send a suitcase with all of your child's belongings?

- **Stepparents** – What do you want to make sure potential significant others know about your agreement before they decide to become involved as a stepparent? Should stepparents be present at appointments for your child (doctor, school, and so on) without the mutual agreement in advance of the parents? Should stepparents take on the role of exchanging the children? Should stepparents be involved in calling or e-mailing the other household in nonemergency situations without agreement of both parents?

  o Should stepparents schedule appointments for your child? Should stepparents be consulting with professionals for your child without the mutual agreement of both parents? Should stepparents be listed as contacts on important information for your child?

○ What are mutually agreed-upon boundaries both parents want stepparents to respect? Should stepparents talk to your child about subjects such as drugs, sex, religion, and so on? Should stepparents be allowed to discipline your child, and if so, what are the limits?

○ Should your child remain with the stepparent if you are not present to care for your child during your parenting time, or should the coparent be asked first if he or she would like to care for your child? Should your child be allowed to sleep in the same bed with a stepparent whether or not one of the parents is in the bed? How should a stepparent act when the other parent is present?

- **Child Care Expenses** – An important component of a coparenting plan addresses the finances of raising a child. Kids are *very* expensive! Will one parent pay some to the other to cover the child's expenses? Will bills be split or covered by one parent? How will school activities or extracurricular events be covered? What about expenses for extracurricular activities, scholastic events, religious events, and college? How will medical, dental, or optical expenses be covered? Who will cover the health insurance for your child, and how will the cost of the insurance be addressed?
- **Decisions** – Who will make final decisions when all else fails, or what steps will you take before bringing issues to court (for example, will you try mediation)?

The following is a sample of a creative, nonstandard parenting plan. It is not intended to be your parenting plan; in fact, there are items in this agreement that likely will not work for your parenting plan. However, it is an example of how creative your plan can be.

SAMPLE PARENTING PLAN

Our child is entitled to enjoy the following rights:

1. The right to be treated as an important human being, with unique feelings, ideas, and desires, and not as a source of argument between parents.
2. The right to a sense of security and belonging derived from a loving and nurturing environment that shelters him or her from harm.
3. The right to a continuing relationship with both parents and the freedom to receive love from and express love for both.
4. The right to parents who will listen to and show respect for what their child has to say.
5. The right to express love and affection for each parent without having to stifle that love because of fear of disapproval by the other parent.
6. The right to grow and flourish in an atmosphere free of exploitation, abuse, and neglect.
7. The right to know their parents' decision to divorce is not the child's responsibility and he or she will still be able to live with each parent.
8. The right to continuing care and guidance from both parents where the child can be educated in mind, nourished in spirit, and developed in body, in an environment of unconditional love.
9. The right to receive developmentally appropriate answers to questions about changing family relationships.
10. The right to know and appreciate what is good in each parent without one parent degrading the other.
11. The right to have a relaxed, secure relationship with both parents without being placed in a position to manipulate one parent against the other.
12. The right to have one parent not undermine time with the other parent by suggesting tempting alternatives or by threatening to withhold activities with the other parent as a punishment for the child's wrongdoing.

13. The right to be able to experience regular and consistent parental contact and the right to know, in a developmentally appropriate manner, the reason for not having regular contact.
14. The right to be a child and to be insulated from the conflicts and problems of the parents.
15. The right to be taught, according to developmental levels, to understand values, to assume responsibility for his or her actions, and to cope with the just consequences of his or her choices.
16. The right to be able to participate in his or her own destiny.
17. The right not to be used as a messenger or spy between parents.

Residence of the Child

Billy's domicile is restricted to the Arlington Independent School District. Until such time as Billy has his own car and is able to drive, the parents will reside no more than two miles doorstep to doorstep from each other. Once Billy has his own car and is able to drive, the parents will reside not more than ten miles doorstep to doorstep.

Parenting Time Schedule

Failing mutual agreement,

1. General weekly schedule:

Week 1:   The father will be responsible for Billy from the time school is released on Tuesday until 7:30 p.m., when he is picked up by his mother, and from the time school is released on Thursday until school resumes on Friday morning.

Week 2:   The father will be responsible for Billy from the time school is released on Thursday until he returns Billy to his other home at 6:00 p.m. on Sunday.

Beginning when Billy reaches seven years of age and thereafter,

Week 1:   The father will be responsible for Billy from the time school is released on Tuesday until 7:30 p.m., when he is picked up by his mother, and from the time school is released on Thursday until school resumes on Friday morning.

Week 2:   The father will be responsible for Billy from the time school is released on Thursday until school resumes Monday morning (or the next day school resumes if Monday is a holiday).

The mother will be responsible for Billy at all other times not otherwise addressed.

2. Holidays:

Thanksgiving

Each year, the mother's parenting time will begin at 2:00 p.m. the Tuesday preceding Thanksgiving and end at 3:00 p.m. Thanksgiving Day when she delivers Billy to his other home. The father's parenting time will begin at 3:00 p.m. Thanksgiving Day and continue until he returns Billy to his other home at 6:00 p.m. the Sunday following Thanksgiving.

Christmas

Even years – Billy will be with his mother from the time school lets out for Christmas break until 4:00 p.m. Christmas Eve, with his father from the 4:00 p.m. Christmas Eve until 3:00 p.m. Christmas Day, with his mother from 3:00 p.m. Christmas Day until 7:00 p.m. Christmas Day, and then with his father from 7:00 p.m. Christmas Day until school resumes after Christmas vacation.

Odd years – Billy will be with his father from the time school lets out for Christmas break until 4:00 p.m. Christmas Eve, with his mother from 4:00 p.m. Christmas Eve until 3:00 p.m. Christmas Day, with his father from 3:00 p.m. Christmas Day until 7:00 p.m. Christmas Day, and then with his mother from 7:00 p.m. Christmas Day until school resumes after Christmas vacation.

Spring break
Odd years – Billy will be with his father from the time school is released for spring break until the time school resumes.

Even years – Billy will be with his mother from the time school is released for spring break until the time school resumes.

Father's Day / Mother's Day
Billy will be with his father from the time school is/would be released for Father's Day weekend until the time school resumes.

Billy will be with his mother from the time school is/would be released for Mother's Day weekend until the time school resumes.

Monday federal holidays and other days school is not in session
If a school or federal holiday falls on a Friday, Billy's time with the parent whose parenting time is on the weekend will begin on Thursday when school is released. If a school or federal holiday falls on a Monday, Billy's time with the weekend parent will end when school resumes on Tuesday.

If the parent who has parenting time with Billy on a federal holiday has to work on that federal holiday and that parent does not take the day off but the other parent is off work, the parent who is off work shall have the right to parenting time with Billy beginning at the time that Billy's school begins and ending at 7:00 p.m. that same day, provided that the parent who is exercising parenting time with Billy on the federal holiday picks up Billy from the other parent's residence and the other parent picks up Billy from the parent's residence at 7:00 p.m.

Independence Day
Even years – Billy will be with his mother from 7:00 p.m. July 3 until 7:00 p.m. July 5.

Odd years – Billy will be with his father from 7:00 p.m. July 3 until 7:00 p.m. July 5.

Halloween-
Odd years – Billy will be with his mother from the time school is/would be released for Halloween until the time school resumes/would resume the following day.

Even years – Billy will be with his father from the time school is/would be released for Halloween until the time school resumes/would resume the following day.

The parents agree when possible they will both take Billy trick-or-treating together.

Summer
Prior to age ten, Billy will continue the regular school schedule with the exception that the father may elect by May 1 fourteen consecutive days of parenting time during the summer, provided it does not interfere with any otherwise addressed parenting time. The mother May elect by May 15 seven consecutive days of parenting time, provided it does not interfere with any otherwise addressed parenting time.

At and after age ten, Billy will continue the regular school schedule with the exception that the father may elect by May 1 fourteen consecutive days of parenting time during the summer, provided it does not interfere with any otherwise addressed parenting time. The mother May elect by May 15 fourteen consecutive days of parenting time, provided it does not interfere with any otherwise addressed parenting time.

Children's/Parent's Birthdays

Billy will be with his father from the time school is/would be released for the day before his father's birthday until the time school is/would be released the day following his father's birthday.

Billy will be with his mother from the time school is/would be released for the day before his mother's birthday until the time school is/would be released the day following his mother's birthday.

On his birthday, Billy will be with the parent who would not have parenting time with him from the time school is/would be released until 6:00 p.m., when he is returned to his other home.

3. Additional Topics

1. The parents will not schedule activities for Billy during the other parent's parenting time without the advance mutual agreement of the other parent.
2. To the best of their ability, the parents will not involve or let Billy overhear conversations about possible schedule changes for parenting time without the advance consent of the other parent.
3. The parents will maintain the same sleep routine until such time as both parents mutually agree otherwise.
4. The parents will encourage Billy to call the other parent each night to say goodnight until otherwise mutually agreed upon.
5. Prior to any significant changes in Billy's physical appearance, both parents must mutually agree upon on such changes.
6. Dating provisions:
   a. The parents must actively date a significant

      other no fewer than six months prior to introducing that person to Billy.

b. The parents will not introduce Billy to a significant other prior to seven months after the final decree is signed by the judge.

c. For the following six weeks after Billy's initial introduction to a significant other, all meetings between Billy and the significant other will be with a parent and in a public location.

d. After the six weeks of Billy's introduction to a significant other, the relationship between Billy and that person will grow at a gradual pace.

e. During a parent's parenting time, his or her significant other will depart the home, hotel room, or other sleeping location of Billy or his parent prior to Billy going to bed and will not return until after Billy wakes up in the morning for at least a period of six months after the introduction to Billy.

7. The parents will allow Billy to refer to a stepparent by any respectful terms (such as the stepparent's first name, Stepmom/Stepdad, or Mom/Dad) that Billy is comfortable with, without influence of either parent or any stepparent.

8. The parents will not leave Billy unsupervised until Billy reaches an age mutually agreed upon by the parents and for durations agreed upon by the parents.

9. If a parent will not be available for eight hours or more during his or her parenting time, that parent will offer the other parent the first right to care for Billy over all other individuals, including relatives. The parent offering the first right to care will specify the hours of care needed, and may elect another person to care for Billy if the other parent is not available during those hours. The parent accepting the first right will be responsible for picking up and returning Billy at the hours designated by the requesting parent. The parents will not ask each other why they are being offered the first right, but

instead will simply accept or deny the opportunity. This agreement does not apply:

   a. To travel or when there are family functions and events such as weddings, funerals, or reunions.

   b. When Billy is engaged in activities with peers at his initiated request, such as a peer sleepover.

10. If Billy will be out of the local area for one night or more, the parent who has arranged the travel will provide the other parent Billy's travel itinerary prior to departure.

11. Either parent may call, e-mail, or text Billy during Billy's time with his other parent during reasonable hours and at a reasonable volume per day.

12. Billy will be allowed to call, e-mail, or text either parent during reasonable hours and at a reasonable volume per day.

13. Both parents will support both maternal and paternal extended family relationships with Billy, independent of either parent's parenting time.

14. Each parent will notify the other parent within twenty-four hours of the time they schedule or are notified of any medical, psychological, scholastic, or extracurricular appointments for Billy, or immediately if twenty-four hour notice is not available. Each parent will also notify the other parent of any schedule changes or cancellations.

15. The parents must mutually agree on all extracurricular activities prior to consenting to Billy participating in them and/or enrolling Billy in extracurricular activities, withdrawing Billy from agreed-upon activities, or not taking Billy to such activities once Billy has been enrolled.

16. The parents will not, nor will they allow others to, purchase a cell phone for Billy until such time as both parents mutually agree on the phone and guidelines for phone usage.

17. The parents will establish mutually agreed upon Internet guidelines prior to allowing Billy to access the Internet.

18. Each parent will "cc" the other parent during e-mails to professionals about Billy.

19. The parents will not, nor will they allow others to, disparage the other household members in the presence or hearing range of Billy.

20. The parents will not, nor will they allow others to, discuss matter relating to litigation, child support, or court services in the presence or hearing range of Billy.

21. The parents will not, nor will they allow others to, use Billy as a messenger to deliver verbal messages or physical items between the parents.

22. The parents will not, nor will they allow others to, probe Billy about his time at his other home or about coparenting matters.

23. The parents will use two-home friendly vocabulary (such as "parenting time" or "when you are in your other home" or "when you are with your mother") with Billy and in Billy's presence rather than words such as "possession," "custody," or "visitation."

24. The parents will use a behavioral plan between both homes to address unacceptable behaviors and consequences for these behaviors, and will use carry-over discipline between homes.

25. Information that is readily available (such as online school information) is the responsibility of that parent to gather. Information that either parent receives that is not readily available to the other parent will be provided to that other parent in a timely manner (such as school-picture order forms).

26. The parents will maintain www.ourfamilywizard.com accounts to communicate in writing as needed, solidify agreements, maintain a calendar, manage Billy's expenses, and detail his professional contacts.

27. The parents will not ask Billy where he wants to live or encourage Billy in any way to choose between his parents, but will help Billy understand he has two homes.

28. Billy will be allowed to carry his property between homes. However, both homes will maintain

primary-care items, such as clothes, hygiene items, and over-the-counter medicines, so that Billy does not have to carry these items.

29. Prior to seeking further nonemergency litigation over coparenting matters, the parties will use alternative dispute-resolution options.

30. The parents will, and will instruct others to, follow the coparenting plan.

For more information about developing parenting plans and parenting plan schedules, as well as other free literature, visit:

www.afccnet.org/resourcecenter/resourcesforfamilies/

Chapter 13: Behaviors That Put Children in the Middle

When children are growing up between two homes or have parents residing between two homes, there are some worrisome behaviors that often develop without appropriate parenting, and parents may not recognize the warning signs of such behaviors. The following information will address some of the common mistakes coparents make when raising children between two homes.

Many times, parents may not even recognize that they are putting their children in the middle by making these mistakes. It's hard to stop what you don't know is a problem in the first place. By identifying these twenty-two areas, I hope that I am helping to protect your child from being in the middle. It was my recognition of these behaviors that led to the initial development of this book.

Mistake 1: Triangulation

Triangulation occurs when parents involve their child in parental decision-making or negotiations rather that maintaining communication between the adults. For example, suppose your child refuses to have time with his or her other parent, talk to the other parent on the phone, or bad-mouths the other parent. When you say, "I can't make my child go to his other home if he doesn't want to go," or "It's between them," or if you leave it up to the child to return the other parent's calls, your behavior puts the child in the position of being able to make adult decisions.

In other words, instead of the adults making the decisions

in a straight line between each other and then informing their child of the decision, or seeking input from the child only after both parents agree, the child is allowed to make direct decisions with one parent about the child's relationship with the other parent. In such a situation, a child may try to play a parent against the one that he or she is upset with.

The following is an example of healthy coparenting. Decisions are made between the parents, and the child is involved only with the agreement of both parents.

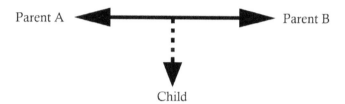

The following is an example of triangulation. Decisions are made between the parents and child, with little or no communication between the parents.

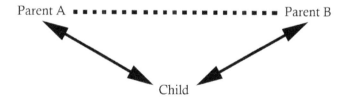

The following is an example of extreme triangulation (parental alienation, which is discussed later in this chapter). One parent is cut out of communications completely, and may have no access to the child.

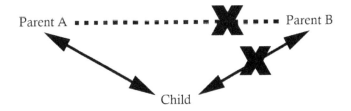

Parent A ■ ■ ■ ■ ■ ■ ■ ■ ■ ■ ■ **X** ■ ■ ■ ▶ Parent B

Child

Mistake 2: Divided Loyalties

Emotionally healthy parents encourage a child's relationship with both parents and all the child's emotionally healthy family members. Think about the "my" child example from the "Litigation Thinking" section in Chapter 3.

Divided loyalties occur when a child tells each parent different and opposing things about what he or she wants, needs, or wishes for. If your child is experiencing divided loyalties, often your child is trying to please both parents and is telling each parent what he or she thinks that parent wants to hear. In more extreme situations, your child may even tell each parent that the child wants to "live" with just that parent.

Mistake 3: Projection

Projection, also called mirroring, occurs when a child bases his or her behavior on how the child interprets his or her parent is handling a situation. Often, a parent reporting the stress of a child has difficulty seeing that the child is acting on that parent's own anxiety.

Before assuming that your child is having difficulty adjusting or assuming that the problem is with the other household, you should ask yourself how you are feeling, and what you are thinking about the two-home situation, your coparent, and the schedule between homes. A projection reaction may be apparent during exchanges in which the child is fine ten minutes after the exchange, but during the exchange has tantrums or displays separation anxiety.

Mistake 4: The Choice of "Where to Live"

Imagine being asked or encouraged to pick between the two most important people in your life. If you haven't watched the movie Sophie's Choice lately, you might want to watch it. Unfortunately, while parents usually agree that their daughter should not have the right to choose to live with her boyfriend or their son shouldn't be moving in with his friend's cool parents, some parents bring their children into the conflict between parents by asking their children to choose who to live with. Or they will tell their children that they will be a more active parent if the children decide to live with him or her.

Sometimes parents are threatened by a child's relationship with the coparent or want their child to want only the one parent. The parent may feel this way because he or she is unable to separate his or her own feelings from the child's, expecting the child to parrot the parent's own feelings, such as anger toward their coparent. Rather than viewing the child as having two homes, that parent "wins" if the child lives with him or her. If the child lives with that parent, that parent is "in control" of the child. Sometimes a parent may not be as active in his or her child's life as he or she could be, so the parent views having the child live with him or her as a way to be more active in the child's life rather than taking the time to be more involved in other ways, such as going to the child's school and having lunch with the child.

Remember, your child has two homes. If your child wants to spend more time in one home or the other occasionally, then let him or her. For example, it's likely that on Christmas Day, your child will want to spend time in both homes. Give your child the freedom to enhance his or her relationship with both parents, rather than keeping a rigid schedule. If your child wants to spend more time with you, then have lunch with your child at school, be active in field trips, and/or coach his or her team. Make a point to be more active in your child's life even when it is not your parenting time.

Mistake 5: The Secret-Agent Child

The secret-agent child reports between two homes, or is probed about what happens in his or her other home with questions such as, "Where did you go? What did you do? What did you eat? What did you watch? Who did you see it with?"

Often, parents will tell others, "I don't ask my children; they just tell me." However, parents often give their child more attention when their child shares something that is not that parent's business or when their child says something negative about his or her other household. For instance:

- While you are doing the dishes, you give your daughter only half of your attention and minimal eye contact until she mentions, "Mommy met Bob at the pool."
- Suddenly your daughter becomes the center of your universe. You turn down the faucet or turn it off. You turn to your daughter and look her in the eyes. You ask, "Who is Bob?"

Guess what your child has just learned?

To get your full attention, I need to share private information about my other parent, or I need to complain about my other parent.

If you are going to ask your child questions, ask your child about his or her time with you instead of your child's time with the other parent. For example:

- Instead of "What did you eat?" ask "What would you like to eat?"

155

- Instead of "Where did you go?" ask "Where would you like to go?"
- Instead of "What did you watch?" ask "What would you like to see?"

IMPORTANT: If your child makes an outcry about abuse, please call your state's child-protective services and take your child to a counselor who is trained to talk to your child as a neutral party. Don't be tempted to probe. If there is actual abuse or neglect, your unskilled probing may have unintended consequences, such as derailing or damaging any investigation, or lead to a finding that you manipulated your child's story and clouded the child's report.

Mistake 6: The Messenger Child

The messenger child is used by the parents to communicate with and/or deliver items to each other rather than each parent taking responsibility to communicate with the other household. Phrases such as, "Tell your mother I won't be picking you up next Tuesday," or "Tell your father you need to go to bed by nine," or "Give this to your mother," place the child in the position of messenger. This places a burden and unnecessary responsibility on the child. For example, the mother is angry because the father is running late and the child then feels guilty because he or she recalls the father told the child to tell the mother he would run late next week. Children also fail to give correct facts, may not have all the facts, or may not be developmentally able to retain or convey the facts.

If there is information you need to give the other parent, call, fax, e-mail, text, or send a letter, but don't use your child to fulfill your responsibility to get information to the other parent. If there is something you need to deliver to the other parent, hand it to him or her yourself or mail it, but please do not give it to your child to deliver by placing it in his or her backpack or handing it to your child.

Mistake 7: The Secret-Keeper Child

If there is something happening or you are making decisions you do not want the other parent to know about, do not expose your child to that event or situation. It is a huge burden for children to keep secrets between homes. Think about the impact of asking a child to lie to or keep secrets from the other parent. In the long run, you are teaching your child that it is okay to lie and keep secrets from *you*.

One way to put your children into the roles of secret keeper, secret agent, and then messenger is for your child to experience a situation where you know the other parent would be concerned, then not tell the other parent. Your child:

- Starts off as the secret keeper.
- Becomes the secret agent when your child is probed after accidentally revealing to the other parent the situation, and may be further probed because the other parent is concerned about safety or a violation of an agreement between the parents.
- Becomes the messenger by relaying the information about the event the other parent should have been told about by the parent who involved the child in the first place.

Mistake 8: Involving Your Child in Adult and Legal Issues

There is adult business and there is child business. Children, from toddlers to teens, should be shielded from adult business. Adult business can be a huge burden for a child to carry. Adult business as related to coparenting includes:

- What happened during court, mediation, or collaborative-law meetings.

- What was said and specific details in the development of the parenting plan.
- Child support.
- Other coparenting financial matters.
- Copies of the court order.
- The intimate relationship between the adults and any negative history between them.
- The schedule between the homes, unless otherwise previously agreed upon by both parents.

For example, you get tickets to a local theme park and they are good only next weekend, which happens to fall on the other parent's parenting time. Do not involve your child in the situation. Contact the other parent, explain the situation, and see if he or she will allow your child to go with you or if he or she is willing to trade time. If your coparent has something else equally important planned or is stuck in the rigid thinking addressed in Part 1 of this book, offer him or her the ticket so that your child does not miss out on the opportunity. But do not tell your child, "Ask if your mom will let you go," or "I would have taken you, but your dad refused to let me."

Mistake 9: The Exchange-Facilitator Child and Conflict During Exchanges

In some cases, the adults do not want to see each other at exchanges, so their child is forced to assume the role of the exchange facilitator. For example, some parents pull up curbside and blow their car horn, make a call, or send a text to notify their children they are there to pick the children up.

Think about this. How would you respond if your daughter's boyfriend pulled up curbside and blew his horn at your daughter, instead of coming to the front door to pick her up? Or called you and said, "Send your daughter out here, I'm waiting"?

When exchanges occur at either home and everyone

chooses to be civil for the child, I recommend that the exchanges should be made inside each of your child's homes. This is how you would handle it if your child had only one home and a relative was taking your child somewhere. You would invite the relative in, talk about your child, make sure your child had everything he or she needed, and then you would send them on their way. However, if domestic violence is involved, curbside or public exchanges may be needed.

Sometimes parents will use business locations or the police station to exchange children. Unfortunately, if there is bad traffic or an accident, these children are stuck waiting in a car. If it's about equal travel time, one parent could deliver and the other parent return rather than meeting halfway. You will use the same amount of gas.

No matter how you handle the exchanges, children do not need to be exposed to conflict or the emotional burdens of their parents. During the few minutes it takes to exchange your child between parents, focus on being a role-model parent. To do this, you need to love your child more than you may feel angry, sad, or frustrated with the other parent. Focus on being a coparent rather than an "ex." Generally, it is better to discuss coparenting issues prior to or after the exchange, rather than during the exchange.

Mistake 10: "I Miss You"

Certain phrases that adults use in conversations with their child may create unintended emotional burdens for a child growing up between two homes. For example:

- "I'll miss you."
- "I missed you when you were gone."
- "I sure do miss you."
- "I can't wait to see you. I feel so sad when you are gone."
- "Your puppy really cries for you when you are gone."

Phrases such as these can make your child feel guilty about enjoying time at his or her other home or with other family members. Rather than saying, "I miss you," I recommend you say, "I love you," which is what you are really trying to tell your child anyway. Other phrases that do not induce guilt include, "I'm happy when I think about you," or "I know you like spending time over there, and I feel good about that." If your child tells you, "I missed you," first remember who trained them to say that, and then respond, "I thought of you too, and I felt happy every time I did."

On this same note, I realize it is often difficult to tell your child goodbye during exchanges. Keeping your chin up and being emotionally strong for your child will help him or her during this transition.

Mistake 11: Parentification

Changing your parenting behavior from your previous parenting style, altering the child's role, and/or relying on the child to meet your needs are all examples of parentification. Parentification burdens a child with developmentally inappropriate responsibilities.

When parentification occurs, the child takes on the responsibility of taking care of one or both parents or taking care of younger children. The child may be encouraged or expected to provide physical or emotional support to a parent or to take on the responsibilities of a parent.

An example of parentification occurs when a parent starts sleeping with a child who has not slept with parents before the separation. The parent will claim the child now needs someone to sleep with because the child is having a difficult time adjusting. Often it is actually the parent who wants someone to sleep with, or who wants to be needed by the child. This sleeping arrangement may change again once a significant other begins spending the night.

Other examples include parents using phrases such as:

- "Now that Dad's gone, you're the man of the house."

- "You take such good care of me, and your brother and I really appreciate that, now that there isn't another woman in the house."
- "You're not just my child, you're my best friend."
- "Your dad has a new relationship, but I don't have anyone but you."
- "I'm going to miss you so much when you are gone. I just don't know what I'll do without you."
- "Your mother used to take care of all those things. I just don't think I can do it. Can you?"
- "I know you want to spend time with your friends, but I only get you every other weekend, and I want all your time to be spent with me."

Do not lean on your child for emotional support. You need to let your child know you are going to take care of him or her, and that he or she is not responsible for taking care of you.

Mistake 12: Splitting Siblings

Be cautious when considering splitting siblings. For example, "you take the boys, and I'll take the girls." While children may not have the benefit of having continuous access to the parental relationships as they would if they lived in one home, the one continuous relationship they can have is with their siblings.

When children remain on the same schedule as their siblings, they learn to work through conflict, lean on each other, and share in experiences. There may be times, especially if there is an age gap between the children, when the children are split for activities and events. However, following a plan between two homes where the siblings spend less time with each other on a regular schedule can diminish their sibling relationship. Many siblings fought like cats and dogs as children, but are best friends and there for each other as adults because of the bonds they created as children working through family issues.

Mistake 13: Negative Comments and/or Body Language

When you are angry or frustrated, it can be difficult to fight the urge to say negative things about the other parent to your child. However, your child is worth your biting your tongue.

When you criticize the other parent in front of your child, your child may internalize a message that part of him or her is bad. If your child hears you call his or her father an "idiot," the child may think, "Part of me is an idiot." Negative comments about the other parent also put a child in a bind, where the child wonders whether he or she can express affection for the other parent.

Be careful to monitor how you answer the phone when your coparent calls; there is a big difference between, "Hey, what's up," versus "What do you want now?" Your child benefits from knowing he or she has permission to continue loving and respecting both parents. You give this permission not only by explicitly telling your child that he or she has permission to love you both, but also by keeping negative comments and tones to yourself.

Sometimes words are not needed; children can and do pick up on negative body language. In fact, ignoring your coparent at functions, not saying positive comments about him or her on a regular basis, or using body language that displays your dislike for your coparent can speak more loudly than words. Rolling your eyes when speaking about the other parent, pointing your finger at your coparent, holding your arms in a defensive manner when speaking to your coparent, or leaning forward in an attacking way are examples of negative body language.

You also need to be careful not to inadvertently criticize the other parent within hearing range of your children. If your child overhears you criticizing the other parent to your attorney, friends, or family, it is just as hurtful as you criticizing the other parent directly to your child.

Where do children overhear negative comments? Here are some examples:

- "I was making a peanut butter and jelly sandwich in the kitchen when Mommy's attorney called and I heard her talking bad about Daddy."
- "Dad thought I was in my bedroom. But I was really in the living room, and then my grandma showed up, and they were talking about how bad Mom is."
- "I was walking by my mommy's and stepdaddy's room, and even though the door was closed, I could hear them saying how bad my daddy is."

The other place children are exposed to negative comments is on the Internet, often through social media. When you post something negative on the Internet about your coparent or your child's other home, it is difficult to completely remove it from the Internet. In fact, it is incredibly easy for your child, their friends, and your child's other family members to find this information.

If your case were to go to court, consider what a judge would think of you if you were disparaging your coparent on the Internet and how that behavior reflects on your ability to put your child's needs first. I recommend that you not post anything on the Internet that you do not want your child to read or that you do not want to have to defend before a family-law judge.

Lastly, in this era of technology, it is easy for children to read text messages or otherwise be exposed to unhealthy coparenting matters. Think about this before you leave your cell phone, laptop, desktop, or tablet available to your child.

Mistake 14: Allowing Others to Make Negative Comments

Aside from you, who else should not make negative comments about your coparent?

For starters, your child. When two parents live together, if their child were to criticize one of the parents, they'd reprimand the child. And yet, when parents separate, instead of saying, "Don't say those things about your father," parents respond, "Why baby, what did he do to you this weekend?" Or even worse, "You're right. That's why I divorced her."

You also need to make sure the other adults in your inner circle do not make negative comments about your coparent or the members of your coparent's household. The adults in your inner circle include your extended family members, significant others, spouses, neighbors, and friends. Try to educate these individuals about the damage done to your child if they continue this behavior and give them a copy of the coparenting supporters versus coparenting detractors page from Chapter 3. If they refuse to stop, be sure to protect your child from these individuals.

Mistake 15: Involving Your Child's Events or Professionals

When you are at an extracurricular activity for your child, who are you there for? Of course, the answer should be your child.

However, if you are at the event talking to the person next to you about how rotten your coparent is, what happened in the divorce process, or how much you hate your coparent's new love interest, who are you really there for? The answer would be yourself. You are exploiting your child's extracurricular activity, making the event about your desire to vent rather than about celebrating your child, and exposing anyone in hearing range to your coparenting conflict. Those conversations need to be kept away from your child's activities.

A child may tell their friend, "I didn't know your parents were divorced." That friend responds, "Yep, but I don't talk about it much." To which the other child responds, "Well your mom sure does. I just heard her in the bleachers telling my mom all about it."

What does the child think when he or she hears this? Maybe something like: *My parents got a divorce and all I got was this lousy T-shirt.* In such a situation, you appear to be parading the divorce and coparenting conflict all around the child.

If a person the child is close to passes away, if a pet dies, or when a large change occurs in a child's life such as two parents separating, it is important to inform the professionals that are a part of your child's life. However, when you try to involve the coach or folks in the bleachers in "your side" of the story, you are bringing the conflict to the children. Teachers in these situations have told me that they are forced to have two parent-teacher conferences instead of one because the parents refuse to sit in the same room to hear about their child, but both parents want to pull the teacher into their side of the story.

Another example of involving professionals for the child occurs when parents call the police when there is no danger to either the parent or the child. Think of the message it sends to your child when he or she sees a police officer attempting to regulate the unhealthy behaviors of the parents.

In cases I have been involved in, police have been called because the parents disagreed over who should pick up their child from the school, or the parents have exchanged the child at the police station, or the police have been called because a parent did not have the parenting skills to send the child out to the other parent.

Obviously, if you or your child are at risk of abuse, your child benefits from knowing the police are there to protect him or her. However, when the police are called in over simple coparenting matters, you are not only putting others at risk by inappropriately exhausting police resources, but you are also demonstrating a lack of control that may increase the likelihood your child will not feel secure in either parent's care.

Allow the professionals and paraprofessionals for your child to focus on your child, rather than on the coparenting situation. Often parents who develop a successful coparenting relationship will hear from others, "I didn't even know you were divorced. You all get along so well and work so well together."

Mistake 16: "I Always Tell My Child the Truth"

I have heard parents involve the children in adult business with the excuse, "But I always tell my child the truth."

There are many truths we protect children from, such as the details of "how they were made." You may tell them different things at different ages, but at no point are you going to say, "We were feeling feisty in the backseat of the car..."

Think about it. Do you want to know all the intimate details of your conception?

I sometimes hear parents with anger-control issues say, "Well, if you leave me, I'm going to tell the children the truth, that you left me." Of course, what they don't want revealed to the child is why the other parent left them.

Parents may say, "When you're old enough, I'll tell you why we got a divorce." That's not a good idea. Instead, in regard to a separation, remember the appropriate phrases discussed in Chapter 7. What your child needs to hear is, "Mom and Dad tried to work it out, but we couldn't. We will always love and care for you."

Mistake 17: Your Child's Property

Your child's two homes should have all the underwear, toothbrushes, socks, and over-the-counter medication that your child will need for the entire time he or she is there. Your child should not have to carry those things back and forth but should be allowed to carry what he or she wants. Children living in two homes have a right to their belongings just like children who live in one home.

If you won't let your child carry what he or she wants, be honest at Christmas and label the present under the tree with, "To Billy, to borrow in this household." In dysfunctional coparenting situations, children sometimes have to use a checklist to check off things they could not care less about, such as underwear, and they are not allowed to carry what they want between homes.

Unfortunately, some parents even mark children's clothing with an "M" or a "D," identifying it as "Mom's clothes" or "Dad's clothes." I recommend both households keep ample clothes for your child and let those clothes belong to your child. If your child comes over in one pair of jeans and comes back in another pair, then the child still has jeans.

Security and attachment items such as security blankets, stuffed animals, and other items that comfort your younger child should be exchanged between homes along with the child. For your older child, you may want to duplicate some items between the homes, such as computers, video game systems, or bicycles. These items would be difficult or too fragile to transport back and forth on a regular basis. But in general, I encourage you:

- To let your child take what he or she wants to.
- Do not have your child pack items you should already have in his or her home with you.
- Do not treat your child's items as your items.
- If your child forgets to bring something, return the child to your coparent's home to get the item he or she forgot, or if you are the parent with the item, deliver the item to the child.

Mistake 18: Pets

Often during the separation period, parents try to cut costs, such as the expenses related to a pet. It is hard enough for your child to leave each of you behind on a regular basis. Getting rid of a family pet your child cared for will only add to the grief and difficulty your child is experiencing during the transition.

This is also not a good time to add a new pet to the mix. During the turmoil of a recent family separation, it can be much more difficult for a child to leave a new pet behind. I recommend waiting a good deal of time after the separation before you buy a pet that your child has to leave behind.

If possible, see if you and your coparent can agree to allow your child to carry any pets between homes. And if you know the other parent is allergic to cats, dogs, or hamsters, I encourage you not to bring such a pet home for your child. The allergens on your child and his or her items will not serve to improve your child's time in his or her other home.

Mistake 19: Pressure to Conceal Feelings

Forcing your child to conceal his or her feelings about your coparent or the persons in the other home can create a tremendous burden on your child. Children often tell parents what they think their parent wants to hear. When your child is afraid that his or her affection for your coparent will make you feel sad, angry, or jealous, your child will often cover up his or her feelings of love for the other parent to meet what your child sees as your needs.

Children can never have too many people who love them, want to care for them, and want to protect them. Allow your child the freedom to develop his or her own feelings about your coparent and the individuals in your child's other home.

Mistake 20: Rigidity

As I detailed in Chapter 4, your child will benefit from some flexibility in the schedule as needed. Your child has two homes that can work together, and I encourage you to make flexibility the "norm" regarding time with both parents.

Flexibility allows for family changes, significant events, your child's special activities, and family trips. Being flexible as coparents can make it possible for your child to have Christmas in both homes on one day or to have peer activities independent of parenting time. Most importantly, flexibility makes it easy for your child to ebb and flow between homes.

Mistake 21: Alienating Behaviors

Alienation occurs when a parent manipulates or brainwashes a child against the other parent, or against people associated with the other parent, such as a stepparent. Alienating behaviors, whether intentional or unintentional, are a form of child abuse. In some cases, both parents engage in these behaviors.

An alienated child may exhibit any of the following behaviors:

- Freely expressing intense dislike or hatred toward the rejected parent.
- Resisting or refusing contact with the rejected parent.
- Using trivial or false reasons to justify his or her hatred.
- Talking openly to anyone about the rejected parent's perceived shortcomings.
- Speaking glowingly about the favored parent in contrast to giving extremely negative views of the rejected parent.
- Appearing rehearsed and brittle in interviews.
- Giving stories about the rejected parent that have no depth and are wooden and repetitive.
- Not expressing any ambivalence or guilt about his or her behavior toward the rejected parent.
- Projecting hatred of the rejected parent to extended family and pets.

Examples of alienating parental behaviors include:

- Referring to their coparent only by his or her name, and teaching the child that this is how he or she too should address the parent. For example, "Susan is coming to get you," "John is here," or "Mr. Smith called and said he is on his way," instead of "Your mom is coming to get you," "Your dad is here," or "Your daddy called and said he is on his way."

- Dressing the child down and drawing attention to exchanges. For example, "You better put on your faded clothes because you tend to get dirty over there," or "We're going to put these clothes on that are too small so maybe your mother will get you new clothes."

- Derogatory probing. For example, "They just fed you junk food again this weekend, didn't they?" or "She seems to like your stepbrother more than you, doesn't she?"

- Sharp division of clothes, toys, and property. The children are not allowed to carry their own things between homes, and can use some things only when they are with one parent.

- Restricting phone and email access. For example, telling the other parent, "You can't call because it's my time," as if children stop having a mother because it's their time with their father or vice versa. Another example is giving the child the choice to talk to or return a call to the other parent.

- Becoming overly enmeshed (homeschooling to keep the other parent out of the "school," seeing themselves as a best friend to the child instead of as a parent, pushing the stepparent as the *new* parent). These parents believe that because they feel a certain way, the child must also.

- Seeing things in "black and white" and therefore setting up a belief that one parent is "good" while the other is "bad."

- Repeating negative comments about their coparent that the child may come to believe over time.

- Making excuses for inexcusable behaviors when it comes to the child talking about or interacting with the other parent. For example, the alienating parent will not tolerate the child calling him or her by an inappropriate term, but will allow the child to refer to the other parent that way.

- Implying that their coparent or their coparent's significant other is dangerous in some way. For example, a mother may tell her young daughter to sleep with her cell phone when she is in her other home so she can call 911. Some parents inform their child that the other parent will kidnap him or her one day.

- Engaging in a campaign of denigrating behavior or questioning—did you get enough to eat, was he/she mean, they seem to love your stepbrother more than you, and so on.

- Claiming that their child has separation anxiety but it occurs only prior to going to the other parent, not with friends or other family members.

- Interrupting the child's time with the other parent in many different ways. For instance, emailing, calling, or texting several times a day to check on the child. This increases the child's anxiety about the other parent and can make the child feel guilty about going to his or her other home.

- Teaching the child that the coparent is "totally unacceptable" by not allowing the other parent to come to the front door or into the child's room. The young child learns that the other parent may "contaminate" the home or that this parent cannot be trusted.

- Trying to rewrite reality, or challenging the child's factual recollection of events.

- Magnifying their coparent's flaws. For example, if the coparent is depressed, the alienating parent tells the child that the coparent is mentally ill. If the coparent drinks occasionally, the alienating parent may refer to him or her as an alcoholic.

- Using negative terms, such as "adulterer," "abandoner," or "liar," to describe the other parent. Sometimes these parents are distorting the truth. Sometimes these parents are telling the actual truth, but without considering the impact on or inappropriateness of adult information for a child.

- Involving the child in adult matters.

- Forming alliances with one child over the other,

particularly the same sex child or an older child.

- Creating friction with the other parent's new significant other and exacerbating the child's negative perception of the new significant other.

- Openly blaming the coparent for the failed marriage or the divorce, even in the presence of the children. Such parents often take no responsibility for their own role in the failure of the marriage.

- Destroying all reminders of the other parent. May even destroy pictures of the child's extended family.

- Tending to use "us" language with regard to the divorce. "Your mother is divorcing us!" Or "Your father is going to beat us in court next week!"

- Making loaded comments before a reluctant child leaves for his or her other home. Such as, "I feel so bad that you have to go," "I've done everything I can to protect you from these visits, but the courts don't care what you want," or "Just be brave and know that am praying for you." Sometimes these parents claim that they encourage their child to have fun during "visitation." Even so, the negative messages will speak the loudest.

- Using guilt and manipulation to force their child into picking sides. These parents may make comments such as, "I have nothing; your mother has everything!" or "I miss you so much when you're with your father. I hate being alone."

- Playing the victim role to gain a child's affection and pity. These parents put out messages that say, "Poor me, it's all your mother's/father's fault."

- Using their voicemail or caller ID to screen all calls from their coparent and not letting the child talk to the coparent. This includes restricting the child's phone and e-mail access to the other parent. Again, this teaches the child that the unacceptable parent is "bad" and should be avoided. It also teaches the child that any feelings of wanting to contact the other parent are "wrong."

- Claiming that they want the child to enjoy the other

parent but doing or saying subtle things to interfere in the children's relationship with the other parent.

- Making it known, directly or indirectly, that to defend or to love the other parent may cost the child their affection. It's all or nothing. Such parents use fear to force their child to be loyal.
- Refusing to let the child bring home anything from the other parent's home or sharply dividing clothes, toys, or property.
- Making negative comments around the child, but claiming they're just joking.
- Minimizing the significance of their alienating behaviors.
- Without the consent of the other parent, scheduling events for the child that interfere with the child's time with the other parent, or creating conflict between the child and the other parent.
- Making excuses for their inability to parent by letting the child "drive the bus."
- Using religious beliefs to alienate the child from the other parent. For example, "Your mother is evil because she wants a divorce," or "Your father will burn in hell, so we must pray for him every night."
- Repeatedly pointing out how they have been the "devoted parent," the "trustworthy parent," or the "dependable parent." Even without criticizing the other parent directly, these parents are implying that the other parent is unacceptable.
- Alienating mothers may encourage their children to use their maiden or new last name instead of their father's last name.

Dr. Richard Warshak describes alienated and alienating parenting as follows:

- **The rejected** (alienated) parent may contribute to the problems by parenting in a harsh and rigid style. Personal characteristics of the rejected parent may include passivity or withdrawal in the face of conflict; immature or self-centered behavior in relation to the child; angry, demanding, or intimidating character traits; a lack of empathetic connection to the child as a separate individual; and/or angry and counter-rejecting behavior toward the alienated child. This type of parenting requires intensive parenting education and/or counseling in order to change behaviors.

- **The favored** (alienating) parent may believe that the child does not need the other parent. He or she may also portray the rejected parent as dangerous, and describe the rejected parent as not loving or caring for the child. In a small number of cases, the alienating parent may even make false accusations of abuse. More often though, the alienating parent focuses on exaggerating the deficits of the other parent.

In *Divorce Casualties: Protecting Your Children From Parental Alienation*, Douglas Darnall (1998) identifies three types of alienating parents:

- **Naïve Alienators** – These parents are ignorant of what they are doing but are willing to be educated and to change.
- **Active Alienators** – These parents lose control of appropriate boundaries when triggered; they "go ballistic." When they calm down, they don't want to admit that they were out of control.
- **Obsessed Alienators** – These parents operate from a delusional system where every fiber of their being is committed to destroying the other parent's relationship with their child.

Although *Between Two Homes* focuses on building a successful coparenting relationship and recommends that you never disparage the other parent in the hearing range of your child, there may be some extreme cases that merit exceptions to this general recommendation. For example, if you are dealing with an alienated child, you may need to explain certain circumstances to your child, use constructive disapproval, or even defend yourself. Such discussions should be conducted with the supervision of a skilled mental-health professional. If you are the alienated parent, you may want to consult with a therapist who specializes in reunification therapy to guide you through the process of repairing your relationship with your child.

If you are concerned about becoming alienated from your child, I strongly recommend that you visit the website of Dr. Richard Warshak at warshak.com. His book, *Divorce Poison: How to Protect Your Family from Bad-mouthing and Brainwashing,* and helpful tools, such as the video "Welcome Back Pluto," are valuable resources for the alienated parent and child.

Mistake 22: Estrangement

There are valid reasons why a child may not want to spend time with a parent. If a parent is dangerous, abusive, negligent, or otherwise impaired in their parenting, a child will likely not feel safe or desire to spend time with that parent.

Estrangement occurs when a parent engages in behaviors that discourage his or her child from wanting to spend time with that parent. For example, the estranged parent may:

- Be physically, sexually, or mentally abusive to the child in the home or over the phone/Internet.
- Be physically, sexually, or mentally abusive to others in the home and the behavior is witnessed by the child.
- Allow others to physically, sexually, or mentally abuse the child or others in the home.
- Bad-mouth or allow others to bad-mouth the other parent.
- Be neglectful.
- Have abandoned the child in the past.
- Be overly punitive and punish the child with severe

and chronic rigidity.
- Be chemically dependent.

If you have estranged yourself from your child, there are options available to you. You may consider:

- Taking live or online parenting classes.
- Taking anger-management classes.
- Attending reunification therapy with your child.
- Referring back to the "Special Topics" section in Chapter 3.

Chapter 14: To Do's

I hope the best for your family and that this book helps you look at situations from a different point of view. I also hope this book provides you with some new tools for your successful coparenting relationship. Please keep the following pointers in mind:

- Maintain a businesslike coparenting alliance.
- Create a two-home environment.
- See things through your child's point of view, not yours.
- Ask yourself, "How would we have handled this if we lived together?"
- Make sure your family and friends behave in an emotionally healthy manner.
- Remind your child that he or she is not to blame.
- Reassure your child that he or she is loved in both homes.
- Allow your child the freedom to love his or her other parent and family members in the other home.
- Provide stability.
- Maintain flexibility between homes.
- Expect that your child's behavior will change.
- Keep your child out of the conflict.
- Seek help from qualified professionals if necessary.

Recommended Reading
for Adults

Considering Divorce?: Critical Things You Need to Know
by Melinda Eitzen, Joanna Jadlow, and Brenda Lee Roberts. Covers the entire process, from making the decision and the various divorce methods available, to moving out of the house. This book includes chapters on a variety of common situations and misconceptions about divorce.

Cooperative Parenting and Divorce: Shielding Your Child from Conflict
by Susan Blyth Boyan and Ann Marie Termini. An easy-to-read parent workbook that provides vital information and gives real-life examples and worksheets so parents may practice new skills that shield their child from parental conflict.

Divorce Poison: How to Protect Your Family from Bad-mouthing and Brainwashing
by Richard A. Warshak. Divorce Poison is a time-tested work that gives parents powerful strategies to preserve and rebuild loving relationships with their children, and provides practical advice from legal and mental-health professionals to help their clients and safeguard the welfare of children.

Feeling Good: The New Mood Therapy
by David D. Burns. This book helps you free yourself from fears, phobias, and panic attacks; overcome self-defeating attitudes; and unleash your potential for success.

Helping Your Kids Cope with Divorce the Sandcastles Way
by M. Gary Neuman, with Patricia Romanowski. Dozens

of special activities and fun exercises that will help you communicate and get closer to your child.

How to Avoid the Divorce from Hell: And Dance Together at Your Daughter's Wedding
by M. Sue Talia. Full of practical suggestions for getting through a divorce while doing the least possible damage to your children.

Joint Custody with a Jerk: Raising a Child with an Uncooperative Ex
by Julie A. Ross and Judy Corcoran. This hands-on, practical guide offers many proven communication techniques that will not only help you deal with a difficult coparent by describing examples of common problems, but also teach you how to examine your roles in sticky situations.

Parents Are Forever
by Shirley Thomas. This book is full of advice based on your child's specific age group.

Splitting: Protecting Yourself While Divorcing Someone with Borderline or Narcissistic Personality Disorder
by Bill Eddy and Randi Kreger. Splitting is an essential legal and psychological guide for anyone divorcing a "persuasive blamer": someone who suffers from conditions such as borderline personality disorder or narcissistic personality disorder.

Voices of Children of Divorce
by Dr. David Royko. Quotes from children of divorce.

Recommended Coparenting Websites

www.betweentwohomes.com — Parenting education, coparenting classes, literature, and links to other online resources. You will also find printable pages from this book, such as the Rules for Coparenting and Guidelines for Effective Emails Between Homes.

www.afccnet.org — Information about parenting plans and other online resources.

www.comamas.com — Support for parents and stepparents.

cooperativeparentingblog.com — The Cooperative Parenting Institute promotes the healing and enhancement of family relationships.

www.internetvisitation.org — "Virtual visitation" is the use of electronic communication tools, such as e-mail, instant messaging, video conferencing, video calls, video mail, and so on, to coordinate communication between parents and children.

www.kidsstay.org — Information for parents moving between homes about how to allow their child to stay in one home.

www.ourfamilywizard.com — Online tool for managing expenses, communication, parenting-time schedules, children's activities, and other important information.

www.uptoparents.org — A free, confidential, and interactive website for divorcing and divorced parents.

www.sharekids.com — A secure "coparenting assistant" program designed to minimize conflicts between separated and divorced parents who are sharing custody of their children.

Books for or About Children

Meet Max: Learning About Divorce from a Basset Hound's Perspective
by Jennifer Leister. Meet Max allows children to identify with a family pet who is experiencing emotions and sharing concerns they may recognize in themselves. Meet Max is meant to be read together by parents (or other family members) and their children who are affected by divorce.

Divorced But Still My Parents: A Helping Book About Divorce for Children and Parents
by Shirley Thomas. For children ages six to twelve. This book addresses the five stages of grief through the story of Kristen, a kitten whose parents are divorcing.

The Boys and Girls Book About Divorce
by Richard A. Gardner. Dr. Gardner offers warm reassurance and honest answers to questions frequently asked by children of divorced parents.

It's Not Your Fault, Koko Bear
by Vicki Lansky. For children ages three to seven. This book addresses divorce issues through the story of Koko, a bear whose parents are divorcing. It's a read-together book with instructions and considerations for parents.

Families Are Forever!
by Melissa Smith. A child-friendly, interactive workbook that encourages children to use artwork as a means to express their feelings about divorce-related transitions.

Dear Mr. Henshaw
by Beverly Cleary. For older children. This book provides a

great model of a way to release emotions: through writing. The book depicts a child going through divorce writing to Mr. Henshaw about how he feels. A Newbery Medal-winning book!

Don't Fall Apart on Saturdays! The Children's Divorce-Survival Book

by Adolph Moser. When their parents divorce, children often feel their world is falling apart. In this book, Dr. Moser discusses the traumas that children experience, and in a friendly, caring manner, he offers information that can help young people through their troubled times.

Mom's House, Dad's House for Kids

by Isolina Ricci. An inside view of separation, divorce, and forming a stepfamily. This book is primarily for children ten and older to read alone or with their parents and is meant to be an encouraging and realistic resource that empowers children with practical ways to gain understanding, perspective, and self-knowledge.

Bibliography

Ahrons, C. (1994). *The Good Divorce: Keeping Your Family Together When Your Marriage Comes Apart.* New York: HarperCollins.

Amato, P. R. (2000). "The Consequences of Divorce for Adults and Children." *Journal of Marriage and the Family* 62: 1269–1287.

Amato, P. R. (2006). "Marital Discord, Divorce, and Children's Well-Being: Results from a 20-Year Longitudinal Study of Two Generations." Pp. 179–202 in Alison Clarke-Stewart and Judy Dunn (Eds.), *Families Count: Effects on Child and Adolescent Development.* New York: Cambridge University Press.

Amato, P. R. and Afifi, T. D. (2006). "Feeling Caught Between Parents: Adult Children's Relations with Parents and Subjective Well-Being." *Journal of Marriage and the Family* 68: 222–235.

Amato, P. R., and Cheadle, J. (2005). "The Long Reach of Divorce: Divorce and Child Well-Being Across Three Generations." *Journal of Marriage and the Family* 67 (1): 191(106.

Amato, P. R., and Gilbreth, J. (1999). "Nonresident Fathers and Children's Well-Being: A Meta-Analysis." *Journal of Marriage and the Family* 61: 557–573.

Amato, P. R., and Maynard, R. (2007). "Decreasing Nonmarital Births and Strengthening Marriage to Reduce Poverty." *The Future of Children* 17(2): 117–141.

Amato, P. R., and Rezac, S. (1994). "Contact with Nonresidential Parents, Interparental Conflict, and Children's Behavior." *Journal of Family Issues* 15 (2): 191–207.

Appel, A. E., and Holden, G. W. (1998). "The Co-Occurrence of Spouse and Physical Child Abuse: A Review and Appraisal." *Journal of Family Psychology* 12(4): 578–599.

Appell, J. (2006). *Divorce Doesn't Have to Be That Way: A Handbook for the Helping Professional.* Atascadero, CA: Impact.

Arbuthnot, J., and Gordon, D. A. (1996). "Does Mandatory Divorce Education Work? A Six-Month Outcome Evaluation." *Family Court Review* 34(1): 60–81.

Babcock, J. C., Green, C. E., Webb, S. A., and Graham, K. H. (2004). "A Second Failure to Replicate the Gottman et al. (1995) Typology of Men Who Abuse Intimate Partners... and Possible Reasons Why." *Journal of Family Psychology* 18: 396–400.

Bailey, C.E. (1998). "An Outcome Study of a Program for Non-Custodial Fathers: Program Impact on Child Support Payments, Visitation, and

the Coparenting Relationships." *Dissertation Abstracts International*. UMI
Number: 9939311.

Barker, R. L. (1992). *Social Work in Private Practice*. 2nd ed. Washington,
DC: NASW Press.

Barnard, M., and McKeganey, N. (2004). "The Impact of Parental
Problem Drug Use on Children: What Is the Problem and What Can
Be Done to Help?." *Addiction* 99: 552–559.

Baumrind, D. (1978). "Parental Disciplinary Patterns and Social
Competence in Children." *Youth and Society* 9: 238–276.

Baumrind, D. (1991). "The Influence of Parenting Style on Adolescent
Competence and Substance Use." *Journal of Early Adolescence* 11(1): 56–
95.

Blaisure, K. R., and Geasler, M. J. (2006). "Educational Interventions for
Separating and Divorcing Parents and Their Children." Pp. 575–604 in
Fine, M., and Harvey, J., (Eds.), *Handbook of Divorce and Relationship
Dissolution*. New York: Routledge.

Bohannan, P. (1970). *Divorce and After: An Analysis of the Emotional and
Social Problems of Divorce*. Garden City, NY: Anchor.

Bramlett, M., and Mosher, W. (2002) "Cohabitation, Marriage, Divorce,
and Remarriage in the United States." *Vital and Health Statistics*, Series
23, Number 22. National Center for Health Statistics.

Capaldi, D. M., and Owen, L. D. (2001). "Physical Aggression in a
Community Sample of At-Risk Young Couples: Gender Comparisons
for High Frequency, Injury, and Fear." *Journal of Family Psychology* 15:
425–440.

Cathart, M., and Robles, R. (1996). "Parenting Our Children: In the Best
Interest of the Nation." Report of the U. S. Commission on Child and
Family Welfare Retrieved October 26, 2007 from
http://www.copss.org/research/majority1.htm

Cherlin, A. (2005). "American Marriage in the Early Twenty-First
Century." *Future of Children* 15(2): 33–55.

Clarke, S. C. (1995). "Advance Report of Final Divorce Statistics, 1989
and 1990." *Monthly Vital Statistics Report* 43, 9S. National Center for
Health Statistics.

Clarke-Stewart, A., and Brentano, C. (2006). *Divorce: Causes and
Consequences*. New Haven, CT: Yale University Press.

Chao, R. K. (2001). "Extending Research on the Consequences of
Parenting Style for Chinese-Americans and European-Americans."
Child Development 72: 1832–1843.

Cohen, D. A., and Rice, J. (1997). "Parenting Styles, Adolescent
Substance Use, and Academic Achievement." *Journal of Drug Education*
27: 199–211.

Coley, R.L., and Medeiros, B.L. (2007). "Reciprocal Longitudinal
Relations Between Nonresident Father Involvement and Adolescent

Delinquency." *Child Development* 78: 132–147.

Dalton, J., Carbon, S., and Olesen, N. (2003). "High Conflict Divorce, Violence and Abuse: Implications for Custody and Visitation Decisions." *Juvenile and Family Court Journal* Fall: 11–34.

Darnall, D. (1998). *Divorce Casualties: Protecting Your Children from Parental Alienation.* Dallas, TX: Taylor Pub. Co.

DaVanzo, J., and Rahman, M. (1993) "American Families: Trends and Correlates." *Population Index* 59: 350–86

DeMaris, A. (1992). "Male Versus Female Initiation of Aggression: The Case of Courtship Violence " Pp. 111–120 in Viano, E.C., editor. *Intimate Violence: Interdisciplinary Perspectives.* Washington, DC: Hemisphere.

Dudley, J. (1991). "Increasing Our Understanding of Divorced Fathers Who Have Infrequent Contact with Their Children." *Family Relations* 40: 279–285.

Dutton, D. G., and Nicholls, T. L. (2005). "The Gender Paradigm in Domestic Violence Research and Theory: Part 1: The Conflict of Theory and Data." *Aggression and Violent Behavior* 10(6): 680–714.

Eitzen, M., Jadlow, J., and Lee, B. (2013). *Considering Divorce? Critical Things You Need To Know.* Bloomington, IN: iUniverse.

Ellis, A., and Dryden, W. (2007). *The Practice of Rational Emotive Behavior Therapy.* 2nd ed. New York: Springer.

Emery, R. E. (1994). *Renegotiating Family Relationships: Divorce, Child Custody, and Mediation.* New York: The Guilford Press, p. 13.

Emery, R. E. (2004). *The Truth About Children and Divorce: Dealing with the Emotions So You and Your Children Can Thrive.* New York: Viking.

Emery, R. E., and Forehand, R. (1994). "Parental Divorce and Children's Well-Being: A Focus on Resilience." Pp. 65–99 in Haggerty, R. J., Sherrod, L. R., Garmezy, N., and Rutter, M. (Eds.), *Stress, Risk, And Resilience in Children and Adolescents: Processes, Mechanisms, and Interventions.* New York: Cambridge University Press.

Fabricius, W. V. (2003). "Listening to Children of Divorce: New Findings That Diverge from Wallerstein, Lewis, and Blakeslee." *Family Relations* 52: 385–396. doi: 10.1111/j.1741-3729.2003.00385.x

Fabricius, W.V., and Braver, S. L. (2006). "Relocation, Parent Conflict, and Domestic Violence: Independent Risk Factors for Children of Divorce." *Journal of Child Custody* 3: 7–28.

Federal Interagency Forum on Child and Family Statistics (2007). "America's Children: Key National Indicators of Well-Being." Washington, DC: Federal Interagency Forum on Child and Family Statistics, 2007, VIII Retrieved October 26, 2007, from http://childstats.gov/pdf/ac2007/ac_07.pdf

Follingstad, D. R., Wright S., Lloyd, S., Sebastian, J. A. (1991). "Sex Differences in Motivations and Effects in Dating Violence." *Family*

Relations 40: 51–57.

Furstenberg, F. F., Jr., Nord, C., Peterson, F. J., and Zill, N. (1983). "The Life Course of Children of Divorce: Marital Disruption and Parental Contact." *American Sociological Review* 48: 656–667.

Furstenburg, F. F., Jr., and Cherlin, A. J. (1991). *Divided Families: What Happens to Children When Parents Part.* Cambridge, MA: Harvard University Press.

Furstenberg, F. F., Jr., and Harris, K. M. (1993). "When and Why Fathers Matter: Impacts of Father Involvement on the Children of Adolescent Mothers." Pp. 117–138 in Leman, R., and Ooms, T., (Eds.), *Young Unwed Fathers: Changing Roles and Emerging Policies.* Philadelphia: Temple University Press.

Garber, B. (2008). *Keeping Kids out of the Middle. Child-Centered Parenting in the Midst of Conflict, Separation, and Divorce.* Deerfield Beach, FL: Health Communications.

Geasler, M. J., and Blaisure, K. R. (1999). "1998 Nationwide Survey of Court Connected Divorce Education Programs." *Family and Conciliation Courts Review* 37: 36–63.

Graham-Kevan, N., and Archer, J. (2003a). "Intimate Terrorism and Common Couple Violence: A Test of Johnson's Predictions in Four British Samples." *Journal of Interpersonal Violence* 18(11): 1247–1270.

Graham-Kevan, N., and Archer, J. (2003b). "Physical Aggression and Control in Heterosexual Relationships: The Effect of Sampling." *Violence and Victims* 18(2): 181–196.

Granvold, D. K. (2008). "Constructivist Treatment of Divorce." Pp. 201–226 in J.D. Raskin and S.K. Bridges (Eds.). *Studies in Meaning* (Vol 3). New York: Pace University Press.

Greenberg, S., and Shuman, D. (1997). "Irreconcilable Conflict Between Therapeutic and Forensic Roles." *Professional Psychology: Research and Practice* 1: 50–57.

Gregoire, A., and Manning, C. (2009). "Effects of Parental Mental Illness on Children." *Psychiatry* 8 (1): 7–9. ISSN 1476-1793, 10.1016/j.mppsy.2008.10.012.

Hart, B. (1986). "Lesbian Battering: An Examination." Pp. 173–189 in K. Lobel (Ed.), *Naming the Violence: Speaking Out About Lesbian Battering.* Seattle, WA: The Seal Press.

Hetherington, E. M., and Stanley-Hagan, M. (1999). "The Adjustment of Children with Divorced Parents: A Risk and Resiliency Perspective." *Journal of Child Psychology and Psychiatry* 40(1): 129–140.

Hetherington, E. M., and Elmore, A. (2003). "Risk and Resilience in Children Coping with Their Parents' Divorce and Remarriage." Pp. 182–212 in Luthar, S. (Ed.), *Resilience and Vulnerability: Adaptation in the Context of Childhood Adversities.* New York: Cambridge University Press.

Hetherington, E. M., and Kelly, J. (2002). *For Better or for Worse: Divorce Reconsidered.* New York: W. W. Norton & Co.

Johnson, M. P. (2006). "Conflict and Control; Gender Symmetry and Asymmetry in Domestic Violence." *Violence Against Women* 12(11): 1–16.

Johnson, M. P. (2008). *A Typology of Domestic Violence: Intimate Terrorism, Violent Resistance, and Situational Couple Violence*. Boston: Northeastern University Press.

Johnson M. P., and Leone, J. M. (2005). "The Differential Effects of Intimate Terrorism and Situational Couple Violence." *Journal of Family Issues* 26(3): 322–349.

Johnston, J. R. (1994). "High Conflict Divorce." *Future of Children* 4(1): 165–182.

Johnston, J. R., and Campbell, L. E. G. (1988). *Impasses of Divorce: The Dynamics and Resolution of Family Conflict*. New York: Free Press.

Johnston, J. R., and Campbell, L. E. G. (1993). "A Clinical Typology of Interparental Violence in Disputed-Custody Divorces." *American Journal of Orthopsychiatry* 63: 190–199.

Kelly, J. B. (1993). "Current Research on Children's Post Divorce Adjustment: No Simple Answers." *Family and Conciliation Courts Review* 31: 29–49.

Kelly, J. B. (1994). "The Determination of Child Custody." *Future of Children* 4: 121–142.

Kelly, J. B. (1996). "A Decade of Divorce Mediation Research." *Family and Conciliation Courts Review* 34(3): 373–385.

Kelly, J. B. (2002). "Psychological and Legal Interventions for Parents and Children in Custody and Access Disputes: Current Research and Practice." *Virginia Journal of Social Policy and Law* 10: 129–163.

Kelly, J. B. (2004). "Developing Beneficial Parenting Plan Models for Children Following Separation and Divorce." *Journal of the American Academy of Matrimonial Lawyers* 19: 237–254.

Kelly, J. B. (2007). "Children's Living Arrangements Following Separation and Divorce: Insights from Empirical and Clinical Research." *Family Process* 46: 35–52.

Kelly, J. B., and Emery, R. E. (2003). "Children's Adjustment Following Divorce: Risk and Resilience Perspectives." *Family Relations* 52: 352–362. doi: 10.1111/j.1741-3729.2003.00352.x

Krumrei, E., Coit, C., Martin, S., Fogo, W., and Mahoney, A. (2007). "Post-Divorce Adjustment and Social Relationships: A Meta-Analytic Review." *Journal of Divorce & Remarriage* 46: 145–166.

Kubler-Ross, E. (1974). *Questions and Answers on Death and Dying*. New York: Collier Books/Macmillan.

Lansford, J., Malone, P., Castellino, D., Dodge, K., Petit, G., and Bates, J. (2006). "Trajectories of Internalizing, Externalizing, and Grades for Children Who Have and Have Not Experienced Their Parents' Divorce or Separation." *Journal of Family Psychology* 20: 292–301.

Laumann-Billings, L. and Emery, R. E. (2000). "Distress Among Young Adults from Divorced Families." *Journal of Family Psychology* 14(4): 671–687.

Leon, K. (2005). *Helping Infants and Toddlers Adjust to Divorce*. Columbia, MO: MU Extension.

Leone, J. M., Johnson, M. P., Cohan, C. L., and Lloyd, S. (2004). "Consequences of Domestic Violence for Low-Income, Ethnic Minority Women: A Control-Based Typology of Male Partner Violence." *Journal of Marriage and the Family* 66: 472–491.

Lugaila, T. A. (1992). "Households, Families, and Children: A 30-Year Perspective." *Current Population Reports*, Series, No. 181. Washington, DC: U.S. Government Printing Office.

Macfarlane, J. (2005). "The Emerging Phenomenon of Collaborative Family Law: A Qualitative Study of CFL Cases." Department of Justice Canada. Retrieved October 22, 2007, from http://canada.justice.gc.ca/en/ps/pad/reports/2005-FCY-1.

Magdol, L., Moffitt, T. E., Caspi, A., Newman, D. L., Fagan, J., and Silva, P. A. (1997). "Gender Differences in Partner Violence in a Birth Cohort of 21-Year-Olds: Bridging the Gap Between Clinical and Epidemiological Approaches." *Journal of Consulting and Clinical Psychology* 65: 68–78.

Malone, P. S., Lansford, J. E., Castellino, D. R., Berlin, L. J., Dodge, K. A., Bates, J. E., et al. (2004). "Divorce and Child Behavior Problems: Applying Latent Change Score Models to Life Event Data." *Structural Equation Modeling* 11: 401–423.

Marquardt, E. (2005). *Between Two Worlds: The Inner Lives of Children of Divorce*. New York: Three Rivers Press.

McKay, M., Rogers, P., Blades, J., and Gosse, R. (1999). *The Divorce Book: A Practical and Compassionate Guide*. Oakland, CA: New Harbinger Publications.

McKenry, P. C., Clark, K. A., and Stone, G. (1999). "Evaluation of a Parent Education Program for Divorcing Parents." *Family Relations* 48: 129–137.

McKnight, M. (1991). "Issues and Trends in the Law of Joint Custody." Pp. 209–217 in *Joint Custody and Shared Parenting*. 2nd ed. J. Folberg, ed. New York: Guilford Press.

Migliaccio, T. A. (2002). "Abused Husbands: A Narrative Analysis." *Journal of Family Issues* 23: 26–52.

Nakonezny, P. A., Shull, R. D., and Rodgers, J. L. (1995). "The Effect of No-Fault Divorce Law on the Divorce Rate Across the 50 States and Its Relation to Income, Education, and Religiosity." *Journal of Marriage and the Family* 57: 477–488.

National Center for Health Statistics, (1995). "Births, Marriages, Divorces, and Deaths for April 1995." *Monthly Vital Statistics Report* Volume 43 No. 10: 1–3

Neighbors, B., Forehand, R., and McVicar, D. (1993). "Resilient Adolescents and Interparental Conflict." *American Journal of Orthopsychiatry* 63(3): 462–471.

Nord, C. W., and Zill, N. (1996). "Non-Custodial Parents Participation in Their Children's Lives: Evidence from the Survey of Income and Program Participation." 2 Vols. Final report prepared for the Office of the Assistant Secretary for Planning and Evaluation, U.S. Department of Health and Human Services.

Norton, G. R. (1977). *Parenting*. Upper Saddle River, NJ: Prentice Hall.

Pagani-Kurtz, L., and Derevensky, J. (1997). "Access by Noncustodial Parents: Effects upon Children's Post Divorce Coping Resources." *Journal of Divorce and Remarriage* 27(1/2): 43–55.

Park, H., and Bauer, S. (2002). "Parenting Practices, Ethnicity, Socioeconomic Status and Academic Achievement in Adolescents." *School Psychology International* 23: 386–395.

Peris, T. S., Goeke-Morey, M. C., Cummings, E. M., Emery, R. E. (2008). "Marital Conflict and Support Seeking by Parents in Adolescence: Empirical Support for the Parentification Construct." *Journal of Family Psychology* 22(4) Aug: 633–642. doi: 10.1037/a0012792

Peris, T. S., and Emery, R. E. (2005). "Redefining the Parent-Child Relationship Following Divorce: Examining the Risk for Boundary Dissolution." *Journal of Emotional Abuse* 5: 169–189.

Piaget, J. (1970). *The Science of Education and the Psychology of the Child*. New York: Grossman.

Pollet, S. L., and Lombreglia, M. (2008). "A Nationwide Survey of Mandatory Parent Education." *Family Court Review* 46: 375–394. doi: 10.1111/j.1744-1617.2008.00207.x

Pope, K. S., and Vasquez, J. T. (1998). *Ethics in Psychotherapy and Counseling: A Practical Guide* (2nd ed.). San Francisco, CA: Jossey-Bass Publishers.

Popenoe, D. (2007). "The Future of Marriage in America." *The National Marriage Project*. Retrieved August 27, 2008, from: http://marriage.rutgers.edu/Publications/SOOU/TEXTSOOU2007.htm

Pruett, M. K., Williams, T. Y., Insabella, G., and Little, T. D. (2003). "Family and Legal Indicators of Child Adjustment to Divorce Among Families with Young Children." *Journal of Family Psychology* 17 (2): 169–181.

Pruett, M. K., Ebling, R., and Insabella, G. (2004). "Parenting Plans and Visitation: Critical Aspects of Parenting Plans for Young Children." *Family Court Review* 42: 39–59.

Ricci, I. (1997). *Mom's House, Dad's House: Making Two Homes for Your Child*. New York: Fireside.

Rice, J. (2005). "Divorcing Couples." In M. Harway (Ed.), *Handbook of Couples Therapy*. Hoboken, NJ: John Wiley & Sons.

Riggio, H. R. (2004). "Parental Marital Conflict and Divorce, Parent-Child Relationships, Social Support, and Relationship Anxiety in Young Adulthood." *Personal Relationships* 11: 99–114.

Roth, A. (1976). "The Tender Years Presumption in Child Custody Disputes." *Journal of Family Law* 15: 423–461.

Ruggles, S. (1997). "The Rise of Divorce and Separation in the United States, 1880–1990." *Demography* 34 (4): 455–456.

Rye, M., Folck, C, Heim, T., Olszewski, B., and Traina, E. (2004). "Forgiveness of an Ex-Spouse: How Does It Relate to Mental Health Following a Divorce?" *Journal of Divorce & Remarriage* 41: 31–51.

Salari, S. M., and Baldwin, B. M. (2002). "Verbal, Physical, and Injurious Aggression Among Intimate Couples Over Time." *Journal of Family Issues* 23: 523–550.

Schriver, J. (2004). *Human Behavior and the Social Environment: Shifting Paradigms in Essential Knowledge for Social Work Practice*. Boston: Allyn and Bacon.

Seligman, L. (1996). *Diagnosis and Treatment Planning in Counseling* (2nd ed.). New York: Plenum Press.

Seltzer, J. A., Schaeffer, N. C., and Charng, H. (1989). "Family Ties After Divorce: The Relationship Between Visiting and Paying Child Support." *Journal of Marriage and the Family* 51: 1013–1031.

Steegh, N. V., and Dalton, C. (2008). "Report from the Wingspread Conference on Domestic Violence and Family Courts." *Family Court Review* 46: 454–475. doi: 10.1111/j.1744-1617.2008.00214.x

Steinberg, L., Mounts, N. S., Lamborn, S. D., and Dornbusch, S. M. (1991). "Authoritative Parenting and Adolescent Adjustment Across Varied Ecological Niches." *Journal of Research on Adolescence* 1: 19–36.

Stets, J. E., and Straus, M. A. (1990). "Gender Differences in Reporting Marital Violence and Its Medical and Psychological Consequences." Pp. 151–166 in Straus, M.A., and Gelles, R.J., editors. *Physical Violence in American Families: Risk Factors and Adaptations to Violence in 8,145 Families*. New Brunswick, NJ: Transaction Publishers.

Stolle, D. P., Wexler, D. B., and Winick, B. J. (2000). *Practicing Therapeutic Jurisprudence Law as a Helping Profession*. Durham, NC: Carolina Academic Press.

Stone, G. (2006). "An Exploration of Factors Influencing the Quality of Children's Relationships with Their Father Following Divorce." *Journal of Divorce & Remarriage* 46: 13–28.

Straus, M. A., Gelles, R. J., and Smith, C. (1990). *Physical Violence in American Families; Risk Factors and Adaptations to Violence in 8,145 Families*. New Brunswick, NJ: Transaction Publishers. P. 444.

Straus, M. A. (1997). "Physical Assaults by Women Partners: A Major Social Problem." In Walsh, M.R., editor. *Women, Men and Gender: Ongoing Debates*. New Haven, CT: Yale University Press.

Teyber, E. (2001). *Helping Children Cope with Divorce*. San Francisco, CA: Jossey-Bass Publishers.

Ver Steegh, N. (2005). "Differentiating Types of Domestic Violence: Implications for Child Custody." *Louisiana Law Review* 65: 1379. William Mitchell Legal Studies Research Paper No. 41. Available at SSRN: http://ssrn.com/abstract=910270

Walker, L. E. (1979). *The Battered Woman*. New York: Harper and Row.

Wallerstein, J. S., and Kelly, J. (1980). *Surviving the Breakup: How Children and Parents Cope with Divorce*. New York: Basic Books, Inc.

Wallerstein, J. S., and Blakeslee, S. (1996). *Second Chances: Men, Women, and Children a Decade After Divorce*. New York: Ticknor & Fields.

Wallerstein, J. S, Lewis, J. M., and Blakeslee, S. (2000). *The Unexpected Legacy of Divorce*. New York: Hyperion.

Warshak, R. A. (2002). "Misdiagnosis of Parental Alienation Syndrome." *American Journal of Forensic Psychology* 20: 31–52.

Warshak, R. A. (2010). *Divorce Poison: How to Protect Your Family from Bad-mouthing and Brainwashing*. New York: Harper Collins.

Whiteside, M. F., and Becker, B. J. (2000). "Parental Factors and the Young Child's Post-Divorce Adjustment: A Meta-Analysis with Implications for Parenting Arrangements." *Journal of Family Psychology* 14(1): 5–26.

Winick, B. J. (1996). "The Jurisprudence of Therapeutic Jurisprudence." P. 444 in Winick, B. J., and Wexler, D. B. (Eds.), *Law in a Therapeutic Key: Developments in Therapeutic Jurisprudence*. Durham, NC: Carolina Academic Press.

ABOUT THE AUTHOR

Bradley Craig is a Licensed Social Worker and Certified Family Life Educator. He is a noted coparenting educator in the North Texas area, and has developed a number of parent-education programs for families who are raising children in two homes. He is currently in private practice and at times contracts with organizations to provide services to families. Brad is a trained family-law mediator and provides family-law mediation training with other organizations. In addition, he offers training for other professionals on how to structure approaches to help children being raised between two homes. He works with families who are raising children between two homes and those with continuing custody/parenting-time issues as a Family Mediator, Collaborative Law Allied Professional, Coparenting Case Manager, Coparenting Coach, Educator, Parenting Facilitator, and Parenting Coordinator.

Brad has written the curriculum for several coparenting education programs and has developed several educational videos. He has been a guest speaker on many television and radio programs and is often asked to speak at local, state, and national conferences about coparenting issues. He hosted an ongoing cable television series, The Children in the Middle Show, aimed at educating viewers about both the effects of parental conflict after a separation on children and the services available to help families through coparenting issues.

Brad has two grown sons and resides in Texas with his wife and their dogs.

CPSIA information can be obtained
at www.ICGtesting.com
Printed in the USA
LVHW080334071019
633311LV00008B/67/P